Agricultural Stability
and Farm Programs

Agricultural Stability and Farm Programs

Concepts, Evidence, and Implications

EDITED BY

Daniel A. Sumner

Routledge
Taylor & Francis Group

LONDON AND NEW YORK

First published 1988 by Westview Press

Published 2018 by Routledge
52 Vanderbilt Avenue, New York, NY 10017
2 Park Square, Milton Park, Abingdon, Oxon OX14 4RN

Routledge is an imprint of the Taylor & Francis Group, an informa business

Library of Congress Cataloging-in-Publication Data
Agricultural stability and farm programs: concepts, evidence, and
    implications/edited by Daniel A. Sumner.
        p.   cm.--(Westview special studies in agriculture science
    and policy)
    ISBN 0-8133-7606-8
    1. Agriculture and state--United States. 2. Economic
stabilization--United States. I. Sumner, Daniel A. (Daniel Alan),
1950-   . II. Series.
HD1761.A6224 1988
338.1'873--dc19   88-5654
                                                           CIP

ISBN 13: 978-0-367-01155-0 (hbk)

Contents

Acknowledgments vii

Introduction. ix

1. Instability and Risk as Rationales
   for Farm Programs, *Robert J. Myers
   and James F. Oehmke* 1

   Reaction, *Michael K. Wohlgenant* 23

2. Storage, Stability, and Farm Programs,
   Brian D. Wright 27

   Reaction, *Walter N. Thurman* 51

3. An Analysis of Alternative Market
   and Governmental Risk Transference
   Mechanisms, *Paul L. Fackler* 57

   Reaction, *Kandice H. Kahl* 79

4. Stability and Farm Programs: A Case
   Study of Feed Grain Markets,
   Marshall A. Martin. 85

   Reaction, *Randall A. Kramer* 109

5. Stability and the Tobacco Program,
   Daniel A. Sumner. 113

   Reaction, *Max I. Loyd* 139

6. Stability Issues and Policy Analysis,
   Gordon C. Rausser 143

7. Panel Discussion: Summary and Reactions,
     Bruce Gardner 171

   List of Symposium Participants. 175

Acknowledgments

This symposium was supported in part by The Farm Foundation and the North Carolina Agricultural Research Service, with additional assistance from Resources for the Future.

Thanks to Richard K. Perrin for helping to organize the symposium, and to Erin Newton for editing the conference volume. Ann Phillips also provided useful editorial assistance.

Daniel A. Sumner

Introduction

For many years economists have argued that price and income variability in agriculture are important characteristics of the sector. In fact, this concept has been the intellectual underpinning for most government agricultural regulations and institutions. Stability has been a central topic in public policy towards agriculture at least since the time of the pharaohs. The papers in this volume address several issues related to past and current agricultural policies in the United States.

There are three practical reasons to attempt to understand the economics of agricultural policy. The first is to learn the effects of policies and programs so that we can better project the results of policy changes. Second, if we can understand the forces that determine policy changes, we can anticipate those changes. Finally, understanding the consequences of alternative policies is crucial if we are to design and modify policies that achieve the results we seek.

CAUSES OF VARIABILITY

Crop output varies from year to year in a fashion that is not fully predicted mostly because weather (and hence yield) is variable. All of agriculture depends on biological activity that is inherently vulnerable to weather, disease, and other environmental changes. This intrinsic variability affects both the supply and the demand for farm goods because changes in output in one industry and/or area affect the demand facing other industries and regions. Price variability follows output fluctuations; it is amplified when the supply curve--and even more so, the demand curve--facing an industry is inelastic. That agricultural demand is inelastic has often been asserted and the inelasticity measured. This assertion, however, applies particularly well to aggregate agriculture and not as well to the demand facing a particular crop or region for which reasonable substitutes may be available.

WHY CARE ABOUT VARIABILITY?

The papers in this volume investigate how government policy affects agricultural stability and how fluctuations of agricultural prices and quantities affect policy. Therefore it is useful to investigate, early on, why we care about variability in agriculture. Four distinct reasons to be concerned about the fluctuation over time in economic variables are (1) imperfect substitution of consumption across time, (2) risk aversion, (3) adjustment costs, and (4) costs of mistakes.

Consumption levels at different times are not perfect substitutes. For instance, a good meal tomorrow does not fully compensate for my hunger today. Given equal total consumption, equal distribution over time will be more satisfying than distribution with highs and lows. If our income varies, we will either borrow or save (by storing money or commodities) in order to smooth consumption streams. A fundamental assumption of economics is that marginal rates of substitution diminish for amounts of consumption in different time periods. (The assumption forms the basis for life-cycle or permanent-income models of savings and consumption.) This motive for "stabilization" does not depend on uncertainty; it applies equally when fluctuations are known in advance, as in the case of regular seasonal movements.

Many discussions of stability assume that economic agents have particular forms of risk aversion. Risk and fluctuations over time, however, are related but distinct. Conceptual models of risk relate to alternative levels of income or consumption, not sequences of income. In practice it is difficult to separate a distaste for risk from costs of adjustment or costs of income smoothing. Some activities seem clearly to violate the principle of universal risk aversion. For business firms that may make several investments and for individuals with income from several sources, the case is weak for risk aversion being related to any single enterprise.

Costs of adjustment represent resources used to change production or other activities. Such costs are present even if the changes are fully and correctly anticipated. For instance, before and after each winter, homeowners put up and then take down storm windows. These additional costs of home operation are incurred even though the weather changes are fully expected. (There would be no such costs if it were known that the weather would never change.) It is typically assumed that for a given amount of adjustment, costs of adjustment decrease as the time one has to prepare and carry out the adjustment increases. Thus, in reacting to higher crop prices, a farmer will have lower costs associated with adding land to production if he has a year to prepare rather than a few months. Often when time is short the best response is no response, especially if, for example, high prices are not expected to last.

Costs of misallocation result from the inherent unpredictability of the future. Unanticipated changes in economic conditions imply lower returns, because resources were allocated for conditions that were expected to hold but did not. If a farmer knew exactly what future prices would be, he would never lose money by planting what he discovers to have been the wrong crop for that year. If he knew that prices would never change, he would never be wrong. (Note that unanticipated changes are costly even if there is no distaste for uncertainty per se.)

To assess the costs of adjustment and costs of mistakes caused by the variability of agricultural markets, as well as the scope for possible improvement through stabilization, the extent of adjustment and reactions to variability must be assessed. Variations in yields, prices, costs and revenues require different reactions; different sources of variability allow different degrees of anticipation and compensation. These considerations are consistent with Antle's (1983) analysis of risk in production and lead researchers to examine the alternative markets that farmers and others may use when faced with variable economic conditions.

MEASURES OF VARIABILITY

Most research on stability in agriculture focuses on (1) measures of year to year variability of output price or yield and (2) the impact on producers or consumers. Farm output prices obviously are important to farmers and to buyers, but are not the only variable of interest. For most farms and buyers, many prices of outputs and inputs interact to determine net returns and even the quantities demanded or supplied.

It is natural to use a year as a time unit for analyzing many agricultural issues, but economic decisions may cover much more (or much less) than one year. Intra-year and even year-to-year fluctuations in income flow that do not affect income over the long term are handled with simple borrowing and lending. At most, the costs of adjustment are the interest charges associated with loans taken to smooth the flow. Thus, year-to-year income variance may be of less interest for determining agricultural investment than a measure of variability over a much longer term--given that commercial farmers and agribusinesses typically have access to significant credit lines. In any case, the costs of adjustment would depend on the costs of using various markets and other actions.

Farmers and consumers obviously are not the only agents with interests in agricultural markets. Analyzing stability and policy thoroughly requires consideration of firms and individuals that supply farm inputs and those that market farm outputs. Actions that stabilize one market often destabilize another related market. For example, stabilizing tobacco output prices has resulted in relatively large swings in the demand for tobacco quota and for inputs such as fertilizer and fuel.

INTRODUCTION TO THE PAPERS

The papers included here move from abstract to concrete and from general to specific. Myers and Oehmke consider how variability in agriculture may be a legitimate rationale for policy. They recognize that agents have many alternatives to help deal with variability and suggest that whereas a lack of a complete set of markets for contingent goods may justify government regulation theoretically, real complications of policy design and operation overrule theory. Wright examines programs that use storage as price supports to increase farm incomes. He also notes the importance to price stability of open international markets. Fackler studies the effects of alternative institutions that may stabilize returns when both price and output are random. He focuses especially on the similarities between, and differences in, options and price supports; and he probes the idea of using options instead of government involvement in agricultural stabilization. Next, two chapters consider specific case studies of crop industries that have farm programs with long histories, which usually are justified (in part) by their stabilizing effects. Martin provides policy simulations for the feed grain industry; Sumner shows that the tobacco quota program makes output price less variable on a year-to-year basis but probably has much less impact on other relevant variables. Rausser reviews the major sources of price variability in agriculture and relates them to public policy. He points out the greatly increased variability of world commodity prices, stemming from the use of farm programs to insulate domestic markets from shifts in world supply and demand.

The papers in this volume attempt to contribute to a fuller understanding of agricultural markets and policy. They do not provide direct solutions to current problems of low prices, high debt, fallen asset values, high budget costs, or increased protectionism. However, better understanding of perennial issues underlying farm problems and policies does contribute to better projections of policy effects, to better forecasts of policy changes, and perhaps to better policy for agriculture.

REFERENCE

Antle, John M. "Incorporating Risk in Production Analysis." American Journal of Agricultural Economics 65(1983):1099-1106.

1

Instability and Risk as Rationales for Farm Programs

Robert J. Meyers
and James F. Oehmke

ABSTRACT

It is often argued that farmers face extraordinary instability and risk and that this causes economic inefficiency in agriculture. One implication is that in principle, farm programs can counteract instability and risk, thus improving economic efficiency. But despite all of the attention given to stabilization and risk reduction policies for agriculture, there remains a great deal of confusion over the mechanisms through which instability and risk can lead to economic inefficiency.

The objective of this paper is to outline systematically the ways in which instability and risk can lead to inefficient resource use in agriculture, and hence how stabilization and risk reduction policies may improve economic efficiency. We recognize explicitly that for instability and risk to be sources of economic inefficiency in agriculture, they must lead to some form of market failure. In the paper, we examine three sources of market failure: disequilibrium, incomplete forward markets, and incomplete contingency markets. We claim that these are the only sources of market failure directly associated with instability and risk.

The conclusion is that government intervention in agriculture can, in principle, correct for these market failures but that in practice the potential efficiency gains may be small and are very difficult to realize.

Assistant Professors, Department of Agricultural Economics, Michigan State University. The authors would like to thank Ted Graham-Tomasi and C. Ford Runge for comments on an earlier version of this paper.

INTRODUCTION

It is often argued that farmers face extraordinary instability and risk and that this causes economic inefficiency in agriculture (Schultz, 1945; Johnson, 1947; Hazell and Scandizzo, 1975; Anderson, Dillon and Hardaker, 1977). In principle, farm programs can counteract instability and risk, thus improving economic efficiency. Indeed, this argument is often used to rationalize the existence of farm programs. But despite all of the attention given to stabilization and risk reduction policies for agriculture, there remains a great deal of confusion over how instability and risk can lead to economic inefficiency.

The objective of this paper is to outline systematically the ways in which instability and risk can lead to inefficient resource use in agriculture, and hence how stabilization and risk reduction policies may improve economic efficiency. We recognize explicitly that for instability and risk to be sources of economic inefficiency, they must lead to some form of market failure. In the paper, we examine three ways in which instability and risk can lead to market failure: disequilibrium, incomplete forward markets, and incomplete contingency markets. We claim these are the only sources of market failure directly associated with instability and risk.[1] The conclusion of the paper is that farm programs can, in principle, correct for these market failures but that in practice the potential efficiency gains may be small and are very difficult to realize.

The next three sections contain an overview of the three market failures mentioned above. This is followed by a discussion of whether governments have incentives to correct these market failures when they are found to exist. The paper then concludes with comments on key issues concerning the role of stabilization and risk reduction policies in agriculture.

DISEQUILIBRIUM RATIONALES FOR FARM PROGRAMS

Disequilibrium occurs when prices fail to adjust to differences between quantity demanded and quantity supplied. Thus, markets in disequilibrium are quantity rationed and fail to clear. Furthermore, since resources and commodities are allocated by a rationing mechanism rather than a flexible price system, disequilibrium distorts the ideal market system and leads to economic inefficiency.

Thus disequilibrium may require corrective action from an efficiency-minded government.

Instability in the agricultural sector has been linked directly to the existence of disequilibrium. For example, Schultz (1945) argued that the migration of resources between agriculture and the rest of the economy is inhibited by "rigidities" (disequilibria) in factor markets. In particular he argued that the labor market in the nonagricultural sector is quantity rationed. As a result, any shock or disturbance to the economy cannot be accommodated by a migration of labor from agriculture to industry because of implicit quantity rationing at the rigid nonagricultural wage. Instead, the adjustment has to be borne by agricultural prices and factor returns. Thus, prices are more volatile than they need to be, indicating disequilibria in factor markets.

In modern form, the disequilibrium rationale for government regulation of agriculture is called the fixed-price flex-price model. The idea is that agricultural markets adjust to shocks almost instantaneously but that there are disequilibria in nonagricultural markets which cause nonagricultural prices to be rigid and exhibit "price stickiness" (Bosworth and Lawrence, 1982; Frankel, 1984). Markets with sticky prices are quantity rationed and cannot adjust rapidly to changing economic conditions, thus placing the burden of adjustment on the agricultural markets and their flexible prices. In this case, agricultural markets are called auction or flex-price markets, whereas nonagricultural markets are called customer or fixed-price markets (Okun, 1975).

The existence of both flex-price and fixed-price markets leads to a phenomenon called "overshooting," in which adjustment of agricultural prices to economic shocks is so great that these prices fluctuate beyond their equilibrium levels (Dornbusch, 1976; Rausser et al., 1986). The reason for overshooting is the inability of fixed-price markets to bear any of the adjustment. Thus disequilibrium leads to instability in agriculture, and government intervention may improve efficiency (Rausser, 1985; Frankel, 1986).

Disequilibrium rationales for government regulation of agriculture make the crucial assumption that price instability results from disequilibrium behavior. As a result, standard welfare propositions do not apply and one is left free to argue that any regulation designed to stabilize agriculture close to its "equilibrium path" is clearly justified. Proponents of intervention are thus

released from the burden of justifying intervention on the
basis of a traditional form of market failure, such as an
externality or a public good. Instability is <u>defined</u> to be
market failure, stability becomes an end desired for its own
sake, and stabilization begins to take on a life of its own
as a separate policy objective. This is exactly what has
happened with discussions on stabilization of U.S. farm
programs.

Disequilibrium rationales for government intervention
have been criticized strongly on theoretical grounds
(Sargent and Wallace, 1976; R. Lucas, 1977, 1979). These
authors argue that economic models ought not to violate the
principle that markets clear because the disequilibrium
assumption avoids the fundamental question of why people
would choose not to engage in mutually advantageous trade.
Put another way, disequilibrium models do not have adequate
microeconomic foundations because the cause of the
disequilibrium remains unexplained.

Policy analysis based on models that lack adequate
microeconomic foundations can lead to serious errors and
give an incorrect ranking of policy alternatives (R. Lucas,
1976). Evaluating policies usually involves the difficult
task of determining how people will act in situations that
have never actually been observed. To do this successfully,
one must know not only how past decisions were made but also
how decisions will change as a result of hypothetical
changes in policy. But when markets fail to clear, the
change in behavior will depend not only on the change in
policy but also on whatever quantity rationing is going on.
Thus when disequilibrium is an unexplained postulate rather
than the outcome of an explicit behavioral model, behavioral
responses to policy changes cannot be accounted for and the
task of policy analysis becomes difficult or even
impossible.

The response to these criticisms has been a growing
literature on the microfoundations of disequilibrium
models. This literature generally cites three reasons why
manufactured or consumer goods prices are
sticky: noncompetitive market structures, high costs of
changing prices, and the prevalence of long-term,
fixed-nominal-wage labor contracts in the manufacturing
sector.

Price rigidities result from noncompetitive market
structures when price signals are used to maintain
noncooperative collusive agreements (Stiglitz, 1979). For
example, a collusive agreement may take the form of all
firms setting a single price. If any firm were to charge a

different price, then all firms would behave competitively and lose their share of monopoly profits (Friedman, 1986). Thus each firm has an incentive to maintain its price, even in the face of demand shocks, and some form of quantity rationing will be imposed. Empirical support for this theory is given by Carlton (1986), who found significant price rigidity in some industries and a strong correlation between industry concentration and rigidity.

The second type of microfoundation for sticky prices is that price changes are costly and will be made only when the benefits of changing the price exceed the costs (Mussa, 1981; Taylor, 1979, 1980; Sheshinski and Weiss, 1977). When costs are high it is less likely that prices will respond to a shock to the economy, even if this shock means that there are some benefits to changing a price. This lack of response is exactly what characterizes a sticky or fixed-price market.

The costs of changing prices can include a fixed or "menu" cost, often associated with printing new price lists and menus or retagging consumer items, and a variable cost that is sometimes used to represent the loss of customers due to price increases (Rotemberg, 1982). High menu costs appear to be more important in consumer markets than in agricultural markets because of different trading procedures. Contracts for raw agricultural products are negotiated orally on exchanges such as the Chicago Board of Trade, and changing the price entails little more than calling out the desired price. Changing the prices of consumer goods is more complicated since the prices are usually marked on the items, sometimes indelibly on the container, and packages usually contain relatively small quantities so that a large amount of retagging is required. The implication is that menu costs will reduce price flexibility more in consumer markets than in agricultural markets, resulting in the usual fixed-price flex-price classification. Moreover, it is argued that relatively small menu costs can give rise to price fluctuations of observed magnitudes and to other changes in behavior that cause welfare effects (Akerlof and Yellen, 1985; Parkin, 1986).

The third microeconomic explanation of fixed prices is that the manufacturing sector depends on long-term, fixed-nominal-wage labor contracts. This factor market fixity can lead to rigid output prices in the manufacturing sector and price overshooting in the flex-price sector (Taylor, 1980; D. Lucas, 1986). Most of this literature proceeds from the empirical observation that long-term, fixed-nominal-wage contracts do exist (D. Lucas, 1986; Rotemberg, 1982; Gordon, 1981; Gray, 1976). However, models assuming the existence of fixed-wage contracts do not in themselves provide a microfoundation for sticky prices because they do not explain why agents would agree to a fixed-wage contract (Azariadis and Stiglitz, 1983). Possible microfoundations for fixed-wage contracts have been union intervention (Chen, 1987), asymmetric information between the firm and worker (Gray, 1976), and implicit contracting with asymmetric information (Rosen, 1985).

Despite the significant advances in understanding of the microeconomic foundations of disequilibrium, there are still many problems to be overcome before an adequate theoretical explanation can be claimed. For example, the asymmetric information microfoundations for sticky nominal wages usually assume that each individual's information set is exogenously given (e.g., Townsend, 1982), whereas a satisfactory explanation must realize that each agent endogenously determines his information set based on the expected costs and benefits of acquiring that information. Moreover, once an adequate microeconomic foundation for sticky prices has been found, the implication that price fixity implies market failure may no longer hold. For example, Rosen (1985) finds that the implicit contract labor models "allocate resources through a subtle and 'flexible' nonlinear pricing mechanism, which sometimes gives the outward appearance of rigidities in observed real wages and prices. But these observed rigidities signal little about market failure" (p. 1145).

On empirical grounds, there are arguments both for and against disequilibrium rationales for farm programs. Some argue that there is no sound evidence that disequilibrium is a persistent feature of agricultural factor markets. They point to the massive intersectoral resource adjustments that have occurred--with labor moving out of agriculture and capital moving in--as evidence that disequilibrium is at most a short-run phenomenon (Gardner, 1981). Others argue that persistently low factor returns in agriculture indicate that disequilibrium is pervasive (Brandow, 1977). Additional evidence often cited in favor of disequilibrium rationales for farm programs is the relative variability of agricultural prices as compared to most nonagricultural prices (Andrews and Rausser, 1986) and the relatively rapid response of agricultural prices to economic shocks such as monetary disturbances (Frankel, 1986).

Empirical examinations of labor contracts in manufacturing sectors are consistent with the rigid-wage rationale for the fixed-price flex-price model (Poterba, Rotemberg and Summers, 1986; Rotemberg, 1982; Taylor, 1980; Gray, 1976). However, there is little evidence quantifying the influence of these fixities on commodity prices in either the manufacturing sector or in the agricultural sector. Moreover, the increasing use of cost-of-living adjustments and other indexing arrangements suggests that the prevalence of fixed-nominal-wage contracts is decreasing. We have not been able to find any empirical evidence on the implied efficiency losses in agriculture as a result of sticky manufactured goods prices. Thus, while disequilibrium could theoretically justify farm programs for agriculture, there have been no empirical demonstrations of the benefits that could be expected from such programs or the form that an optimal intervention should take.

INCOMPLETE FORWARD MARKETS

A second reason why an unregulated market economy might fail to be economically efficient is the absence of a complete set of forward markets.[2] Without them, producers and consumers may be unable to coordinate future plans and therefore be unable to allocate current resources and commodities efficiently. That is, the current actions of producers and consumers may be incompatible with markets clearing at all future dates.

There are many forward markets in agriculture, including futures markets and forward contracting. Nevertheless, it is clear that a complete set of forward markets does not exist. Even futures markets only extend a little over a year into the future, and many commodities have neither futures markets nor forward contracting.

When forward markets are incomplete, the way in which forecasts are formed is crucial to the efficiency of resource allocation. One approach to expectation formation is to use temporary equilibrium models (Grandmont, 1977, 1982). In temporary equilibrium models, forward markets are incomplete and forecasts are made in some arbitrary way based on information available at the time decisions must be made. Examples of temporary equilibrium models used extensively in agricultural economics research are the cobweb model (Ezekiel, 1938; Waugh, 1964) and the adaptive expectations model (Cagan, 1956; Askari and Cummings, 1977).

A key feature of temporary equilibrium models is that they have no optimality properties. Since forward markets are incomplete, future plans cannot be coordinated by the price system. And since the rules used to forecast the

future are completely arbitrary, these forecasts also fail
to coordinate future plans. Thus the missing forward
markets and arbitrary forecast rules result in economic
inefficiency. A government equipped with the right model of
the economy could make better forecasts than private
individuals and could therefore intervene in commodity
markets to improve efficiency.

An alternate way of modeling expectations when forward
markets are incomplete is to assume that forecasts are
formed rationally (Muth, 1961; Lucas and Sargent, 1981).
Rational expectations models are a special kind of temporary
equilibrium model identified by a particular
characteristic: instead of forecasts being made using
arbitrary rules, they are consistent with the relevant
economic theory represented by the model. Unlike the case
of arbitrary forecast rules, missing forward markets are not
a source of inefficiency if expectations are formed
rationally. Rational expectations link sequences of spot
markets together in such a way that the missing forward
markets are redundant and full economic efficiency is
obtained (Prescott and Mehra, 1980). This is because future
plans are now coordinated by consensus beliefs about the
true structure of the economy and current actions are
therefore consistent with markets clearing at all future
dates. As a result there is no reason for government
regulation to correct for inefficiencies caused by
incomplete forward markets, as long as individuals have
rational expectations.

On theoretical grounds, the rational expectations
hypothesis has some clear advantages over arbitrary forecast
rules. Arbitrary forecasts ignore the incentives people
have to continue updating forecast rules until all
systematic errors have been eliminated. The incentive to
change forecast rules will persist until forecasts are
correct on average--that is, until forecasts are formed
rationally. Rational expectations is therefore a theory of
optimal forecasting given the economic model under
consideration. Arbitrary forecast rules, such as adaptive
expectations, do not use information efficiently and are
suboptimal in this well-defined sense.

Nevertheless, the rational expectations hypothesis has
not escaped criticism on theoretical grounds. It is
generally agreed that there are strong incentives to use all
available information optimally but the proposition that
this leads naturally to rational expectations has been
refuted (Frydman and Phelps, 1983). The difficulty is that
convergence to rational expectations is problematic and

requires a "consensus condition" which allows people to predict one another's behavior (Frydman, 1982). Without such a consensus condition, different people will base their forecasts on different models of the economy or market and a process of updating forecast rules may never bring convergence to rational expectations (Townsend, 1983).

Empirical studies of the way people actually form expectations when forward markets are incomplete have had mixed results. A recent paper reviewing some empirical evidence concludes that while there are exceptions, "the weight of empirical evidence is sufficiently strong to compel us to suspend belief in the hypothesis of rational expectations, pending the accumulation of additional empirical evidence" (Lovell, 1986). But the results of testing the efficient-markets model of financial asset markets, commodity markets, and foreign exchange markets are less conclusive. For example, Mishkin (1981, 1983) and Fama (1970, 1981) find support for the efficient markets hypothesis, while Leroy and Porter (1981), Shiller (1979, 1981) and Grossman and Shiller (1981) reject the model. However, Flavin (1983) criticizes the variance bounds test used by the latter authors because it is biased towards rejecting the rational expectations hypothesis in small samples. Flavin concludes that the evidence generally supports the rational expectations hypothesis. Other authors (e.g., Hoffman and Schmidt, 1981; Hansen and Hodrick, 1980; Baillie, Lippens and McMahon, 1983) use alternative tests and find mixed support for the rational expectations hypothesis. Baillie (1986) provides a review of the statistical tests used to test rational expectations in exchange markets, and concludes that there is evidence either of the failure of rational expectations or of a risk premium in the market. However, he is unable to determine which conclusion is warranted.

One possible explanation for the discrepancy between these conclusions from tests of the rational expectations hypothesis is the different data sources and test methods. Lovell (1986) relies on survey data, whereas the efficient market model tests rely on market level data. Survey data are often considered unreliable because there are no strong incentives for those surveyed to make and reveal their optimal forecasts. Furthermore, even if some individuals in a market do not have rational expectations, market level data may still be consistent with the rational expectations hypothesis. As long as previously unexploited profit opportunities are removed by the actions of some of the market participants, the market will behave as though forecasts are rational even if some participants are using arbitrary forecast rules.

Even if incomplete forward markets are a source of economic inefficiency in agriculture, a question remains: how large are the resulting economic welfare losses? When forward markets are incomplete and forecasts are not formed rationally, the potential economic welfare gains from intervention equal the value of a rational expectations forecast. A number of authors have estimated economic losses from forecasting errors in agriculture (DeCanio, 1980; Antonovitz and Roe, 1984). DeCanio finds that the value of perfect information to Kansas wheat and corn farmers averaged two percent of gross income over the years 1878 through 1933. Note that this is an estimate of the value of perfect information rather than a rational expectations forecast. Furthermore, a component of the gain to farmers may be a transfer from consumers. Thus, this figure overestimates the net benefit from a rational expectations forecast. Antonovitz and Roe estimate the net benefit to producers and consumers from a rational expectations forecast for the fed cattle market between 1970 and 1980. Their results suggest a benefit of 0.6 percent of gross income from cattle production. As proportions, these benefits appear small.

INCOMPLETE CONTINGENCY MARKETS

When the economy is subject to uncertainty and people are risk averse, then full economic efficiency cannot be achieved without a complete set of contingency markets. That is, full efficiency requires that all risks be insurable given the existing structure of market institutions. Without a complete set of contingency markets, there are insufficient instruments for pooling and transferring risks, and an optimal allocation of risks cannot be attained. Examples of contingency markets are futures markets, options, insurance markets, the bond market, and the stock market.

It is often argued that contingency markets are incomplete even in the most developed market economies (Tobin, 1980). Usual explanations are the high costs of setting up and operating some of these markets and the imperfect information problems known as moral hazard and adverse selection (Arrow, 1986).[3] Recent theoretical advances suggest that call options and subordinated debt instruments may play an extremely important role in completing the structure of contingency markets. For example, Green and Jarrow (1987) show that in principle a firm could complete the market for contingencies associated with its payoffs by a (possibly infinite) sequence of subordinated debt issues. Although subordinated debt instruments are seen frequently in today's economy, and although the number of options markets has been increasing rapidly, the number of commodities or firms for which options or debt markets do not exist remains large. That is, the requirements for providing a theoretically complete set of contingency markets appear to be very strict, and today's economy appears to be a long way from having a complete set of contingency markets.

Government has the potential for improving economic efficiency when contingency markets are incomplete. In this situation, even a rational expectations equilibrium may not be economically efficient, since people cannot trade risks in order to equalize marginal rates of substitution between consumption in any two states of nature. In other words, there is an inefficient allocation of risks. Since government regulations can influence probability distributions on future prices, and therefore marginal rates of substitution between states of nature, a government could improve economic efficiency by policies that reallocate risks throughout the economy (Borch, 1962; Hart, 1975; Newbery and Stiglitz, 1982).

From a theoretical perspective, the incomplete contingency markets rationale for government regulation of agriculture has to be taken seriously. It has sound microeconomic foundations in theories of moral hazard and adverse selection, and a rich body of theoretical research on the properties of incomplete market economies. For example, Geanakopolos and Polemarchakis (1985) show that competitive equilibria exist in incomplete market economies and that such equilibria are indeed inefficient. On the question of whether governments should intervene in incomplete market economies, Arrow and Lind (1970) argue in favor of government investment in risky projects when markets are incomplete, and Mayshar (1977) suggests government subsidization of risky private projects in similar circumstances. Furthermore, Polemarchakis (1979) shows that a regime of price regulation and quantity rationing can dominate competitive equilibria when markets are incomplete.

Direct empirical evidence on whether contingency markets available to agriculture are complete or incomplete is difficult to come by. Unfortunately, one cannot simply scrutinize the structure of existing contingency markets in

search of omissions and imperfections. The fact that
individuals do not trade certain risks is not necessarily
evidence of incomplete contingency markets, because even if
markets for trading these risks were to be introduced, there
might be no use made of them. That is, the "missing"
contingency markets might be redundant and therefore not
required to bring about an optimal allocation of risk
bearing.

To find evidence that contingency markets are
incomplete, farmer and consumer behavior must be examined
for signs of uninsurable risk-taking that influences
resource allocation and consumption decisions. There is a
large body of research on the degree to which farmer
decisions are influenced by uninsurable risks (Anderson,
Dillon and Hardaker, 1977; Young, 1979; Traill, 1978; Myers,
1986). This literature can be interpreted as indirect
evidence that contingency markets in agriculture are
incomplete.

Empirical evidence on the magnitude of economic welfare
losses in agriculture from incomplete contingency markets is
not abundant. Newbery and Stiglitz (1981) have examined the
desirability of international price stabilization schemes in
the presence of incomplete contingency markets. They argue
that gains in economic efficiency would be small and doubt
that governments could actually achieve improvements over
the market mechanism. As a proportion of commodity
revenues, Newbery and Stiglitz find the benefits of price
stabilization to range from 0.2 percent for cotton to 4.1
percent for sugar. As a proportion of income, these
percentages would be even smaller. Myers (1987) has
compared an incomplete markets equilibrium to a complete
markets equilibrium in agriculture. He found that economic
efficiency gains from the best policy--that of introducing a
complete set of contingency markets--are small in relative
terms. The estimated net benefit from complete contingency
markets ranged from 0.02 percent to 0.84 percent of income.
The implication is that no second-best policy designed to
counteract the effects of incomplete contingency markets in
agriculture can significantly improve efficiency. Finally,
Innes (1987) has shown that price support policies in the
presence of incomplete contingency markets can reduce farmer
welfare but increase overall economic efficiency. These
studies are preliminary and further quantification of the
effects of contingency markets and second-best policies are
needed.

GOVERNMENT FAILURE

Market failure creates a potential for improvements in economic efficiency, but there may be little reason to expect governments to formulate policy aimed at realizing these efficiency gains. Policy formation revolves around a complicated system of nonmarket incentives and it is not at all clear that correcting market failures is a primary objective (Peltzman, 1976; Becker, 1983). Furthermore, even when correcting market failures does enter into policy objectives, the incentive structure can distort policy implementation to such an extent that the outcome is less economically efficient that it would have been with the market failure (Buchanan, 1968; Stigler, 1971; McFadden, 1975). This problem has been termed nonmarket or government failure.

Government failure implies that regulation will be oversupplied. Bureaucracies have incentives to maximize budgets and the number of workers they employ rather than to achieve economic efficiency objectives (Mueller, 1979). Furthermore, there is a tendency for technological bias in nonmarket organizations (Wolfe, 1979). In some instances the bias is towards technology as modern, sophisticated technology becomes a symbol of organization performance and a cornerstone of growing budget requests. In other cases the bias is away from technology in order to protect employment numbers. There appear to be few incentives to minimize costs and production may occur inside the production possibilities frontier. Government regulation can have unanticipated negative side effects and can lead to a concentration of power in the hands of a few administrators who are then susceptible to coercion and corruption.

The government-failure literature has led to the view that, far from being an efficient response to disequilibrium and incomplete markets, U.S. farm programs are a mechanism for income transfer to special interest groups that have captured the political process (Rausser, 1982; Oehmke and Yao, 1987). Thus there has been an oversupply of government regulation in agriculture due to the incentive structure facing politicians, bureaucrats and special interest groups. So even if there are serious market failures in agriculture, there may be little reason to expect the political process to result in improvements in economic efficiency.

CONCLUSIONS

Three potential sources of market failure associated
directly with instability and risk in agriculture have been
discussed: disequilibrium, incomplete forward markets, and
incomplete contingency markets. Each incorporates a theory
of how an unregulated agricultural sector may be
economically inefficient, and each has a degree of empirical
support in the literature. This raises three important
questions. First, how large are the potential benefits from
correcting these market failures? Second, are optimal
agricultural policies for correcting these market failures
feasible? Third, is it likely that optimal policies will
result from the political process?

The first question was considered in the discussions
above. The evidence was found to be limited, particularly
in the case of disequilibrium where we could find no direct
empirical estimates. The magnitude of potential economic
welfare gains from correcting for the effects of incomplete
forward and incomplete contingency markets in agriculture
also remains an open question. However, research to date
indicates that the gains may be relatively small.

Optimal agricultural policies for correcting the three
forms of market failure may take many forms. The first best
policy would be to eliminate all sources of disequilibrium
and to introduce missing forward markets and contingency
markets. But governments may find this impossible to
accomplish for the same reasons that private individuals
find it impossible: incomplete information and high
transaction costs.

When first best policies are infeasible, it has been
argued that second best policies are needed to improve
economic efficiency. Second best policies could take the
form of tax-subsidy schemes, price stabilization schemes,
quotas, support price and target price schemes, and so on.
A major problem with such schemes is that they have
prohibitive informational requirements. That is, the
information a government would need in order to design and
implement optimal second best policies is usually
unavailable and extremely difficult, perhaps even
impossible, to obtain.

Consider the case of a tax-subsidy scheme to counteract
the effects of incomplete contingency markets. The optimal
tax-subsidy scheme is a set of payments to or from each
individual that depends, among other things, on the expected
marginal utility of income of all individuals (Newbery and
Stiglitz, 1982). Information on individual marginal

utilities of income will be difficult (impossible?) to obtain. To counteract incomplete forward markets in the absence of rational expectations, governments would need to introduce the missing forward markets or to be able to forecast better than private individuals. But it is hard to see how this might be accomplished. If the government has access to better information than do private individuals, then the optimal policy is simply to make this information available to others. If the government does not have better information, then it is hard to see how an optimal second best policy could ever be implemented.

In the case of disequilibrium, it is difficult even to define what an optimal second best policy would look like. Standard welfare economics does not apply in disequilibrium models, so even defining, let alone implementing, the optimal second-best policy defies standard economic practice. Optimal stabilization of a flex-price sector such as agriculture presumably would require information on the underlying equilibrium path of the sector, information that is exceedingly difficult to obtain.

Turning to the third question, it seems clear from discussion in the previous section on government failure that few incentives exist for governments to undertake policies that correct for market failures in agriculture. Thus, even if optimal policies were feasible and would lead to significant welfare gains (two propositions that have been questioned here), there appears to be little reason to believe that such policies would evolve from the political process.

It would be wrong to suggest that it is logically impossible to design optimal second best, or even first best, agricultural policies to overcome market failures caused by disequilibrium and incomplete markets. But the information requirements of such policies make them very difficult, and perhaps very costly, to design and implement. Furthermore, the potential benefits may not be large. To argue seriously that stabilization and risk reduction policies improve economic efficiency in agriculture, we must be able to say that there is a reasonable prospect of the political process implementing optimal agricultural policies in practice. Currently, this seems to be far from the case.

NOTES

1. There are, of course, other types of market failure besides those listed here (for example, imperfect competition, externalities, public goods, etc.). But these market failures do not relate directly to instability and risk and so are not discussed in the paper.

2. A complete set of forward markets would span all the possible forward claims that agents would wish to write. From a theoretical viewpoint, there is little difference between missing forward markets and missing contingency markets. For interpretive purposes we discuss each type of incomplete market situation separately.

3. Moral hazard occurs when the purchase of insurance induces the insured to undertake risk-increasing actions (or fail to take risk-reducing actions) and these actions cannot be monitored by the insurer. Adverse selection occurs when individuals have different degrees of risk exposure but the insurer cannot distinguish between the different types of individuals. As a result, the same insurance contract must be offered to all individuals. In both cases, the incentives to trade on contingency markets are distorted and may result in no trade on markets that are seriously affected.

REFERENCES

Akerlof, G.A. and J.L. Yellen. "Can Small Deviations from Rationality Make Significant Differences to Economic Equilibria?" _American Economic Review_ 75(1985):708-720.

Anderson, Jock R., John L. Dillon, and J. Brian Hardaker. _Agricultural Decision Analysis_. Ames: Iowa State University Press, 1977.

Andrews, Margaret S. and Gordon C. Rausser. "Some Political Economy Aspects of Macroeconomic Linkages with Agriculture." _American Journal of Agricultural Economics_ 68(1986):413-417.

Antonovitz, Frances and Terry Roe. "The Value of a Rational Expectations Forecast in a Risky Market: A Theoretical and Empirical Approach." _American Journal of Agricultural Economics_ 66(1984):717-723.

Arrow, Kenneth J. "Agency and the Market." _Handbook of Mathematical Economics_, Vol. III. Edited by Kenneth J. Arrow and Michael D. Intriligator. Amsterdam: North Holland, 1986, pp. 1184-95.

Arrow, Kenneth J. and Lind, R.C. "Uncertainty and the Evaluation of Public Investment Decisions." <u>American Economic Review</u> 60(1970):364-378.

Askari, Hossein and John Thomas Cummings. "Estimating Agricultural Supply Response with the Nerlove Model: A Survey." <u>International Economic Review</u> 18(1977):257-292.

Azariadis, Costas and Joseph E. Stiglitz. "Implicit Contracts and Fixed Price Equilibria." <u>Quarterly Journal of Economics</u> 98(1983):1-22.

Baillie, R.T. "Econometric Tests of Rationality and Market Efficiency." Working paper, Michigan State University, 1986.

Baillie, R.T., R.E. Lippens, and P.C. McMahon. "Testing Rational Expectations and Efficiency in the Foreign Exchange Market." <u>Econometrica</u> 51(1983):553-563.

Becker, Gary S. "A Theory of Competition Among Pressure Groups for Political Influence." <u>Quarterly Journal of Economics</u> 98(1983):371-400.

Borch, Karl. "Equilibrium in a Reinsurance Market." <u>Econometrica</u> 30(1962):424-444.

Bosworth, Barry and Robert Lawrence. <u>Commodity Prices and the New Inflation</u>. Washington, D.C.: Brookings Institution, 1982.

Brandow, George E. "Policy for Commercial Agriculture, 1945-71." <u>A Survey of Agricultural Economics Literature</u>, Vol. I. Edited by Lee R. Martin. Minneapolis: University of Minnesota Press, 1977, pp. 209-292.

Buchanan, J.M. <u>The Demand and Supply of Public Goods</u>. Chicago: Rand McNally, 1968.

Cagan, P. "The Monetary Dynamics of Hyper Inflations." <u>Studies in the Quantity Theory of Money</u>. Edited by Milton Friedman. Chicago: University of Chicago Press, 1956, pp. 31-32.

Carlton, Dennis W. "The Rigidity of Prices." <u>American Economic Review</u> 76(1986):637-658.

Chen, Paul. "Wage Changes in Long-Term Labor Contracts." Ph.D. dissertation, Stanford University, 1987.

Cochrane, Willard W. <u>Farm Prices: Myth and Reality</u>. St. Paul: University of Minnesota Press, 1958.

DeCanio, Stephen J. "Economic Losses from Forecasting Error in Agriculture." <u>Journal of Political Economy</u> 88(1980): 234-258.

Dornbusch, Rudiger. "Expectations and Exchange Rate Dynamics." <u>Journal of Political Economy</u> 84(1976):1161-1176.

18

Ezekiel, Mordecai. "The Cobweb Theorem." *Quarterly Journal of Economics* 53(1938):255-280.

Fama, Eugene. "Efficient Capital Markets: A Review of Theory and Empirical Work." *Journal of Finance* 25(1970):383-417.

----------. "Stock Returns, Real Activity, Inflation and Money." *American Economic Review* 71(1981):545-565.

Flavin, Marjorie A. "Excess Volatility in the Financial Markets: A Reassessment of the Empirical Evidence." *Journal of Political Economy* 91(1983):929-956.

Frankel, Jeffrey. "Commodity Prices and Money: Lessons from International Finance." *American Journal of Agricultural Economics* 66(1984):560-566.

----------. "Expectations and Commodity Price Dynamics: The Overshooting Model." *American Journal of Agricultural Economics* 68(1986):344-348.

Friedman, James W. *Game Theory with Applications to Economics*. New York: Oxford University Press, 1986.

Frydman, Roman. "Toward an Understanding of Market Processes: Individual Expectations, Learning and Convergence to Rational Expectations Equilibrium." *American Economic Review* 72(1982):652-658.

Frydman, Roman and Edmund S. Phelps, eds. *Individual Forecasting and Aggregate Outcomes*. Cambridge: Cambridge University Press, 1983.

Gardner, Bruce L. *The Governing of Agriculture*. Lawrence: The Regents Press of Kansas, 1981.

Geanakopolos, John D. and Heraklis M. Polemarchakis. *Existence, Regularity, and Constrained Suboptimality of Competitive Allocations When the Asset Market Is Incomplete*. Cowles Foundation Discussion Paper 764, Yale University, August 1985.

Gordon, Robert J. "Output Fluctuations and Gradual Price Adjustment." *Journal of Economic Literature* 19(1981):493-530.

Grandmont, Jean-Michel. "Temporary General Equilibrium Theory." *Econometrica* 45(1977):533-571.

----------. "Temporary General Equilibrium Theory." *Handbook of Mathematical Economics*, Vol. II. Edited by Kenneth J. Arrow and Michael D. Intriligator. Amsterdam: North Holland, 1982, pp. 879-922.

Gray, Joanna. "Wage Indexation: A Macroeconomic Approach." *Journal of Monetary Economics* 2(1976):221-235.

Green, Richard C. and Robert A. Jarrow. "Spanning and Completeness in Markets with Contingent Claims." _Journal of Economic Theory_ 41(1987):202-210.

Grossman, S. and R. Shiller. "The Determinants of the Variability of Stock Market Prices." _American Economic Review_ 71(1981):222-227.

Hansen, L.P. and R.J. Hodrick. "Forward Exchange Rates as Optimal Predictors of Future Spot Rates: An Econometric Analysis." _Journal of Political Economy_ 88(1980):829-853.

Hart, Oliver D. "On the Optimality of Equilibrium When the Market Structure Is Incomplete." _Journal of Economic Theory_ 11(1975):418-443.

Hazell, Peter B.R. and Pasquale L. Scandizzo. "Market Intervention Policies When Production Is Risky." _American Journal of Agricultural Economics_ 57(1975):641-649.

Hoffman, D.L. and P. Schmidt. "Testing the Restrictions Implied by the Rational Expectations Hypothesis." _Journal of Econometrics_ 15(1981):265-287.

Innes, Robert D. _Government Target Price Intervention in Economies with Incomplete Markets: Welfare and Distribution_. Mimeo, Department of Agricultural Economics, University of California, Davis, 1987.

Johnson, D. Gale. _Forward Prices for Agriculture_. Chicago: University of Chicago Press, 1947.

LeRoy, Stephen and Richard Porter. "The Present-Value Relation: Tests Based on Implied Variance Bounds." _Econometrica_ 49(1981):555-574.

Lovell, Michael C. "Tests of the Rational Expectations Hypothesis." _American Economic Review_ 76(1986):110-124.

Lucas, Deborah J. "Wage and Price Rigidities as Transmissions Mechanisms for Monetary Shocks: Two Dynamic Equilibrium Models." Ph.D. dissertation, University of Chicago, 1986, pp. 19-46.

Lucas, Robert E., Jr. "Econometric Policy Evaluation: A Critique." _The Phillips Curve and Labor Markets_. Edited by Karl Brunner and Allan H. Meltzer. Amsterdam: North Holland, 1976, pp. 7-30.

----------. "Understanding Business Cycles." _Stabilization of the Domestic and International Economy_. Edited by Karl Brunner and Allan H. Meltzer. Amsterdam: North Holland, 1977.

----------. "An Equilibrium Model of the Business Cycle." _Journal of Political Economy_ 83(1979):1113-1144.

20

Lucas, Robert E. Jr. and Thomas J. Sargent, eds. Rational
    Expectations. Minneapolis: University of Minnesota
    Press, 1981.
McFadden, Daniel. "The Revealed Preferences of a Government
    Bureaucracy: Theory." Bell Journal of Economics and
    Management Science 6(1975):401-416.
Mayshar, Joram. "Should Government Subsidize Risky Private
    Projects?" American Economic Review 67(1977):20-28.
Mishkin, Frederic S. "Are Market Forecasts Rational?"
    American Economic Review 71(1981):295-306.
----------. A Rational Expectations Approach to
    Macroeconomics: Testing Policy Ineffectiveness and
    Efficient-Markets Models. Chicago: University of
    Chicago Press, 1983.
Mussa, Michael. "Sticky Prices and Disequilibrium Adjustment
    in a Rational Model of the Inflationary Process."
    American Economic Review 71(1981):1020-1027.
Mueller, Dennis C. Public Choice. Cambridge: Cambridge
    University Press, 1979.
Muth, John F. "Rational Expectations and the Theory of Price
    Movements." Econometrica 29(1961):313-335.
Myers, Robert J. Econometric Testing for Risk Averse
    Behavior in Agriculture. Agricultural Economics Staff
    Paper No. 86-95, Michigan State University, 1896.
----------. The Value of Ideal Contingency Markets in
    Agriculture. Agricultural Economics Staff Paper
    No. 87-13, Michigan State University, 1987.
Newbery, David M.G. and Joseph E. Stiglitz. The Theory of
    Commodity Price Stabilization. New York: Oxford
    University Press, 1981.
----------. "The Choice of Techniques and the Optimality of
    Market Equilibrium with Rational Expectations." Journal
    of Political Economy 90(1982):223-246.
Oehmke, James F. and Xianbin Yao. The Value of Consumers'
    and Producers' Surpluses in Government Policy
    Objectives. Working paper, Department of Agricultural
    Economics, Michigan State University, March 1987.
Okun, Arthur. "Inflation: Its Mechanics and Welfare Costs."
    Brookings Papers on Economic Activity 2(1975):351-401.
Parkin, Michael. "The Output-Inflation Trade-Off When Prices
    Are Costly to Change." Journal of Political Economy
    94(1986):200-224.
Peltzman, Sam. "Toward a More General Theory of
    Regulation." Journal of Law and Economics
    19(1976):211-240.

Polemarchakis, H.M. "Incomplete Markets, Price Regulation and Welfare." <u>American Economic Review</u> 69(1979):662-669.

Poterba, J.M, J.J. Rotemberg, and L.H. Summers. "A Tax-Based Test for Nominal Rigidities." <u>American Economic Review</u> 76(1986):659-675.

Prescott, Edward C. and Rajnish Mehra. "Recursive Competitive Equilibrium: The Case of Homogeneous Households." <u>Econometrica</u> 48(1980):1365-1379.

Rausser, Gordon C. "Political Economic Markets: PERTs and PESTs in Food and Agriculture." <u>American Journal of Agricultural Economics</u> 64(1982):821-833.

----------. "Macroeconomics and U.S. Agricultural Policy." <u>U.S. Agricultural Policy: The 1985 Farm Legislation</u>. Edited by Bruce L. Gardner. Washington, D.C.: American Enterprise Institute for Public Policy Research, 1985, pp. 207-256.

Rausser, Gordon C. et al. "Macroeconomic Linkages, Taxes, and Subsidies in the U.S. Agricultural Sector." <u>American Journal of Agricultural Economics</u> 68(1986):399-412.

Rosen, Sherwin. "Implicit Contracts: A Survey." <u>Journal of Economic Literature</u> 23(1985):1144-1175.

Rotemberg, Julio J. "Sticky Prices in the United States." <u>Journal of Political Economy</u> 90(1982):1187-1211.

Sargent, Thomas J. and Neil Wallace. "Rational Expectations and the Theory of Economic Policy." <u>Journal of Monetary Economics</u> 2(1976):169-183.

Schultz, Theodore W. <u>Agriculture in an Unstable Economy</u>. New York: McGraw Hill, 1945.

Sheshinksi, Eytan and Yoram Weiss. "Inflation and Costs of Price Adjustment." <u>Review of Economic Studies</u> 44(1977):287-304.

Shiller, Robert J. "The Volatility of Long-Term Interest Rates and Expectations Models of the Term Structure." <u>Journal of Political Economy</u> 87(1979):1190-1219.

----------. "Do Stock Prices Move Too Much to Be Justified by Subsequent Changes in Dividends?" <u>American Economic Review</u> 71(1981):421-436.

Stigler, George J. "The Theory of Economic Regulation." <u>Bell Journal of Economics and Management Science</u> 3(1971):3-20.

Stiglitz, Joseph E. "Equilibrium in Product Markets with Imperfect Information." <u>American Economic Review</u>, Papers and Proceedings, 69(1979):339-345.

Taylor, John B. "Staggered Wage Setting in a Macro Model." _American Economic Review_, Papers and Proceedings, 69(1979):108-113.

----------. "Aggregate Dynamics and Staggered Contracts." _Journal of Political Economy_ 88(1980):1-23.

Tobin, James. "Commentary." _Models of Monetary Economies_. Edited by John H. Kareken and Neil Wallace. Minneapolis: Federal Researve Bank of Minneapolis, 1980, pp. 83-90.

Townsend, Robert M. "Optimal Multiperiod Contracts and the Gain from Enduring Relationships under Private Information." _Journal of Political Economy_ 90(1982):1166-1186.

----------. "Forecasting the Forecasts of Others." _Journal of Political Economy_ 91(1983):546-588.

Traill, Bruce. "Risk Variables in Econometric Supply Response Models." _Journal of Agricultural Economics_ 24(1978):53-61.

Waugh, Frederick V. "Cobweb Models." _Journal of Farm Economics_ 46(1964):732-750.

Wolfe, Charles, Jr. "A Theory of Nonmarket Failure." _Journal of Law and Economics_ 22(1979):107-139.

Young, Douglas L. "Risk Preferences of Agricultural Producers: Their Use in Extension and Research." _American Journal of Agricultural Economics_ 61(1979):1063-1070.

Reaction

Michael K. Wohlgenant

The main point made in this paper is that government
intervention can, in principle, correct for market failures
in agriculture arising from disequilibrium, incomplete
forward markets, and incomplete contingency markets but the
potential efficiency gains may be very small and will be
difficult to realize. This is an intuitively appealing
conclusion and I don't have much to add to the authors'
paper except to point out some omissions, the most important
of which, in my estimation, is using only a single criterion
of economic efficiency to justify government intervention.

First, with respect to sources of market failure, the
authors do not include imperfect competition as a type of
market failure because they don't believe this behavior
relates directly to instability and risk. However, as
pointed out by Bieri and Schmitz in a 1974 article in the
American Journal of Agricultural Economics, market
intermediaries can, under certain circumstances, have
incentives to manufacture price instability. Although the
condition under which this will occur--monopsony in the
market for the agricultural product--may not be all that
common, this cause should be included in a complete list of
sources of market failure.

Second, the authors notably exclude, as a source of
price stickiness, inventories held by processors and other
market middlemen. This is generally the case, as Blinder
(1982) and others have shown, and specifically the case as I
have shown in my own work on explaining lags in retail
prices from farm price changes. The implication of my work

Associate Professor, Department of Economics and Business,
North Carolina State University.

is that the fixed-price/flex-price dichotomy can apply to vertically connected commodity markets (from retail to farm) as well as to horizontal nonagricultural and agricultural sectors of the economy.

The main criticism I have of this paper is the single criterion of economic efficiency used to justify government intervention. Myers and Oehmke's paper gives us another reason why government ought not to intervene, not why government does intervene, or why government intervention is more and not less at present. As Rausser (1982) has pointed out, we should enlarge the analytical framework to endogenize government policy. He envisions a model in which a criterion function is defined as a political preference function, with weights on performance measures determined by political economic demand and supply. So a unique political-economic equilibrium can be established in which the marginal rate of political substitution equals the marginal rate of wealth redistribution. Gardner, in a recent article in the Journal of Political Economy (1987), applies Peltzman's theory of efficient redistribution to explaining variations by commodity in producer protection by various farm programs. In his framework, redistribution to producers is measured as gains in economic rents at the expense of taxpayers' incomes and consumers' surplus. Cost of redistribution is deadweight loss, with an efficient redistribution minimizing deadweight losses for a given transfer. He shows that given various measures of degree of government intervention, both political pressure variables and social cost of redistribution are important determinants. An important point here with respect to Myers and Oehmke's paper is that some of their conclusions about the importance or unimportance of different sources of market failure can be reversed when weight is given to political influences.

One final point I would like to make concerns the limitation of public choice considerations to producers' and consumers' surplus. I think it is important to disaggregate consumers into two groups: market middlemen and primary consumers, because market middlemen typically have more political influence through lobbying, etc., and farm price support programs can have different effects on each group. Indeed, many market middlemen possibly benefit, or at worst are no worse off, from policies that raise farm prices. The reason is simple: marketing margins rarely show a tendency to fall when farm prices rise, but more likely show a tendency to rise. Casual evidence in favor of separate treatment of market middlemen lies in the

noticeable lack of organized opposition by market
intermediaries to increased government intervention in
agriculture.

REFERENCES

Bieri, J. and A. Schmitz. "Market Intermediaries and Price
    Instability: Some Welfare Implications." American
    Journal of Agricultural Economics 56(1974):280-285.
Blinder, A.S. "Inventories and Sticky Prices: More on the
    Microfoundations of Macroeconomics." American Economic
    Review 72(1982):334-348.
Gardner, B.L. "Causes of U.S. Farm Commodity Programs."
    Journal of Political Economy 95(1987):290-310.
Rausser, G.C. "Political Economic Markets: PERTs and PESTs
    in Food and Agriculture." American Journal of
    Agricultural Economics 64(1982):821-833.

2

Storage, Stability, and Farm Programs

Brian D. Wright

ABSTRACT

This paper considers the role of storage-based price supports as instruments of farm policy in a changing market environment. A contrast is drawn between the meaning of stabilization in single-period models and in more realistic models with explicit intertemporal links, including storage. In the latter, the distinction between comparative statics and dynamics is crucial. The interpretation of price supports as a means of achieving transfers to producers is properly a question of dynamic incidence. Gains to producers occur as jumps in asset values when a price-support scheme is announced, and these gains are different from those implied in traditional comparative statics calculations.

Other rationales for storage-based price supports are also discussed, including arguments based on their stabilizing effects. In this context, attention is drawn to the interaction of domestic policy with the evolution of the international marketplace.

INTRODUCTION

In looking at the market for major crops in the United States, one might claim that we are now entering the last phase of the second full postwar policy cycle. The first cycle started with the Korean conflict, which sent a demand shock through commodity markets that made prices soar.

Associate Professor, Department of Agricultural and Resource Economics, University of California, Berkeley.
This paper draws heavily on joint work with Jeffrey Williams, who, however, is not responsible for any errors that may be found here.

Price supports were adjusted upward, and as demand subsequently receded, commodity stocks soared; virtually all of the increase was accumulated by the Commodity Credit Corporation (CCC). The United States essentially had ceased to compete on the world market.

With the change in administration in 1960, there was a shift toward a more market-oriented policy. A rapid sell-off of stocks in the major grains occurred during the first half of the 1960s. Lower levels of public stockholding bolstered by substantial acreage diversions persisted until the early 1970s when a combination of production shortfalls and macroeconomic factors increased export demand and reduced public stocks to zero. From then until 1977, the grain markets had no significant acreage diversions or storage interventions.

The high prices of the early 1970s encouraged farmers, policymakers, and many forecasters to believe that the world was entering a period of chronic agricultural scarcity. Loan rates increased sharply between 1975 and 1977 to levels above the market-clearing real price which, as it turned out, had not risen at all and may even have declined since the 1960s. The 1981 and 1985 Farm Bills allowed unrealistic loan rates to persist with only slow reductions and bolstered by very high target prices. The result has been a growing separation of grain production from market forces. Despite the Payment-in-Kind (PIK) program of the early 1980s, there has been a strong buildup of excess stocks similar to that seen in the 1950s; by the 1985 crop year, the ratio of ending stocks to available supply of wheat and corn was similar to that seen around 1960.

We now appear to be starting a reorientation of pricing to meet market competition, as in the early 1960s, with a drastic cut in cropped acreage of over 70 million acres in the coming crop year. There has been some substantial "decoupling" of target prices from producer incentives with the 50-92 provision that allows farmers to qualify for 92 percent of their deficiency payments by planting as little as 50 percent of the program acreage.

The administration is advocating complete decoupling of deficiency payments from production decisions (Economic Report of the President, 1986, 1987). It is also possible that "marketing loans" will be extended to major grains in the near future--in effect, converting the loan program to an additional deficiency payment program. The generic certificates tend to have a similar effect. These measures diminish the support provided by loan programs, although the stocks already accumulated will take some time to dissipate.

We are at a turning point. The evolution of the market over the next several years will depend heavily on tactical policy choices made now--including multilateral decisions made in the new General Agreement on Tariffs and Trade (GATT) round and in other international fora (Rausser and Wright, 1987). Tactics aside, this is a good time to consider longer run policy options and instruments for the next policy cycle. We have the experience of two postwar policy cycles to guide us and the 1985 Farm Bill as a lesson that continuity is not necessarily a low-risk choice.

This paper is intended as a "background contribution" to policy discussion for the next (third postwar) policy cycle that will begin after commodity markets have emerged from their current depressed state. It is not a discussion of future policy design but an overview of the rationale for government storage programs (such as nonrecourse loans and the farmer-owned reserve) and the role of storage as an often chosen instrument of stabilization, price support, and wealth transfer. To narrow the focus of discussion, the paper will concentrate on grain storage. Since the role of a conference paper is presumably to stimulate discussion, I have not hesitated to use conjectures where conclusive evidence or analytical proofs are not at hand.

THE MEANING OF STABILIZATION

Beginning with the seminal work of Waugh (1944), there has been confusion among economists about the meaning of market stability and market stabilization. Waugh concentrated on the variability of price faced by consumers with stable, instantaneously responsive demand. Oi (1961) concentrated on the variability of price faced by producers with stable, instantaneously responsive supply. By concentrating on one side of the market, and by confining their attention to linear curves, both authors were able to consider price and quantity stabilization as two separate manifestations of the same phenomenon of market stabilization. Stability in their analyses means that price and quantity are fixed at their mean values.

When Massell (1969) combined the above analyses to consider both sides of the market, the stabilization of price was attributed to a storage scheme that bought and sold at the mean price. The source of disturbance--a shift in demand or supply--was not affected. Its influence on price was suppressed but the variability of quantity demanded or supplied was consequently greater. If instead the stability were represented by "ideal stabilization," the absence of the fundamental cause of disturbance (for example, weather variation as in Wright, 1979), then price stability could have continued to be consistent with quantity stability. By contrast, the model shows that storage arbitrage does not and cannot stabilize all prices and quantities. In particular, storage-based price stabilization implies increased quantity variation on at least one side of the market. Thus, the first lesson of market stabilization is that, if the fundamental source of market disturbance is not modified,[1] stabilization involves a redistribution of the variability in the market. A decrease in variability of one market measure implies an increase in variability of at least one other measure. The existence of profit-maximizing storage, for example, in a model with a production disturbance tends to increase production variability when supply has positive elasticity but to decrease consumption variability (Wright and Williams, 1982a).

The introduction of explicit storage behavior in the Massell model changes the effects of market disturbances, the role of expectations, and the meaning of instability in that model because storage implies a lag between input decisions (amount put in storage) and sales (amount sold from stocks). Expectations become relevant, and the nature of expectations formation becomes an issue. From the viewpoint of resource allocation, variability becomes uncertainty. Therefore, risk preferences affect allocation; they do not in the Massell model. These effects are also produced by introducing other intertemporal linkages--for example, a lag between production input decisions and outputs, a very realistic assumption for agricultural production; or, indeed, any other production process with inputs that are quasi-fixed.

Finally, with intertemporal linkages formed by storage or lagged effects of inputs, what has happened in the past-- and what is expected in the future--affects the current market equilibrium. This means that when unanticipated policy changes are implemented, the shift to the new stochastic steady state (assuming existence and stability) is not immediate as in instantaneously responsive models (for example, Massell, 1969; Turnovsky, 1976; and many others). Instead, the new policy induces an immmediate jump in asset values and prices followed by dynamic convergence to the new stochastic steady state. The dynamics that have been universally ignored until now are crucial in determining the welfare effects of stabilization policies.

WHY IS STORAGE A POLICY INSTRUMENT?

Since the Great Depression, public intervention in storage has been an important instrument of agricultural policy in the United States. In other major producer-exporter countries (such as Australia, Canada, and Argentina), voluntary public carryovers have not been a prominent part of farm policy. Even though Australian and Canadian wheat exports, for example, are controlled by centralized quasi-governmental marketing boards, there has been no attempt in either country to use inter-year stock management as a major instrument of policy intervention. United States discretionary stocks tend to dominate world holdings.

What is the rationale for U. S. storage interventions? Until recently, virtually all of the literature on market stabilization provided what could be interpreted as an obvious answer (for a recent survey, see Schmitz, 1984). Compared to a market without storage, a market with "public storage" that perfectly and costlessly stabilizes price shows a net welfare gain--a potential Pareto improvement (see, for example, Massell, 1969, and subsequent analytical articles in that tradition). If the government storage authority is efficient and behaves according to socially optimal rules (see Gustafson, 1958a,b; Samuelson, 1971; Wright and Williams, 1982a; and Scheinkman and Schechtman, 1983), government storage must, by definition, be Pareto optimal in an otherwise undistorted market. Compared to a market with no storage, a government buffer stock operating under simpler "price band" rules has also been shown in simulations of numerical cases to provide a potential Pareto improvement over no storage and, in that sense, to increase social welfare.

All of the above results support a common conclusion-- government storage is justifiable if markets are otherwise undistorted, distributional issues (domestic and international) are ignored or solved with lump-sum transfers, and government storage is the only possible type of storage. But why should private storage not be at least as efficient? In much of the literature the question never arises. Where it does, the rationales for public storage intervention shift to other "second best" arguments. Among these are monopoly, lack of public commitment, irrationality, and risk aversion.

Monopoly

The justification for intervention is that private storage would otherwise be monopolized. The inference from legislation in many countries is that the main concern is that monopolists might engage in excessive stockholding in times of scarcity at the expense of consumers. This problem could arise in situations in which demand is linear and price elastic and in which the monopolist owns all production (see Newbery, 1984). But in U.S. agriculture, price inelasticity of farmgate demand is the rule and production is competitive. Under these conditions, a monopolist who controls only storage will store too little, not too much, at all levels of availability (Wright and Williams, 1984a). The evidence suggests that marginal storage costs are constant (Paul, 1970). If so, entry of competitive storers would drive storage rents to zero in the absence of artificial barriers to entry.

Public Inability to Commit Itself Against Future Price-Control Measures

The U.S. government has resorted to grain export embargoes and moratoria to reduce prices during past periods when supply was tight (for example, 1973, 1974, and 1975). Private storers know this, and if they infer that such measures will be repeated, their storage behavior will be affected by the reduction in expected profits. If the government could (and did) plausibly guarantee that it would not repeat such measures in the future, then this would solve the problem. But there is no way that it can do so directly. Storers will expect its behavior to be time consistent. Given storers' expectations and their effect on private storage, future shortages will be even greater, increasing the motivation for such price-controlling actions. In this situation, public storage can help bring total storage closer to the optimal level and reduce fears of future price controls. However, other means of intervention, such as a subsidy to private storage, might be superior. (This problem is discussed at length in Wright and Williams, 1982b.)

Irrationality

If the private sector has adaptive expectations, then a better-informed government can intervene in storage and improve social welfare. Several studies justify government storage on these grounds. To be convincing, such studies should explain why private speculators do not learn as fast as the government and why unexploited private profit opportunities are so hard to find in commodity markets.

The related question of speculative bubbles is more interesting. If they can occur in commodity markets, perhaps public storage intervention could help prevent them. This is an area for theoretical and empirical investigation of the existence of bubbles in markets for major agricultural products and appropriate public response if they do indeed occur. It is not clear that public storage with price floors is such a response.

Risk Aversion of Farmers, Private Storers, and Speculators

Government storage might be optimal as part of a policy package, given the absence of complete markets. Farmers generally are found to be somewhat risk averse, as are consumers. This argument for storage is easy to make but hard to verify. Some caveats are in order. First, price supports do not necessarily make producer income streams more stable. Second, farmers in the United States presumably focus on their net wealth position, not income flows. Risk-reducing responses, such as diversification of the portfolio of assets (including human capital), must be considered. Third, other insurance approaches (such as rainfall insurance) do not appear to have attracted much support from farmers even if offered at rates that are approximately actuarially fair. Fourth, futures markets exist as hedging vehicles that may well be more effective than feasible price-support schemes.

If speculators in futures markets behave in a risk-averse fashion, it is possible that there could be a role for public assumption of risk by intervening in storage markets. According to the Keynesian theory of "normal backwardation" (futures price less than current price in the presence of storage), long speculators (who trade with short hedgers) require a risk premium to compensate them for their role. This risk premium, if it exists in general, is small enough to be difficult to find empirically. Moreover, as Williams (1986) argues, the asset structure for agents likely to take long positions might make such positions risk reducing, in which case long "speculation" may be increased, rather than reduced, by risk aversion. Finally, the observation of backwardation is consistent with risk neutrality and indeed the absence of all market uncertainty (distinguished from price variability) as shown in Wright and Williams (1987).

Market distortions clearly exist, so some second-best rationales can usually be found as a priori justifications for public interventions. However, the rationales listed above do not appear to be compelling. As an alternative to interpreting storage-based price floors as second-best means of market correction by a social welfare maximizing government, we now consider their role as vehicles for transfers in a political market.

THE INCIDENCE OF STORAGE-BASED PRICE-SUPPORT SCHEMES ON PRODUCERS

The entire published literature on the distributional effects of storage schemes on producers has used a comparative statics approach, looking at the effects of stabilization on the steady-state distributions of consumer and producer surplus and net government costs. As shown above, this approach is a satisfactory means of deriving changes in expenditures and income if stabilization occurs (through, for example, modification of weather disturbances where annual weather has no serial correlation) in a model with no storage, no lagged production response, and no other intertemporal links. Then stabilization would imply an immediate shift of regime to a new stochastic steady state.

If the stabilization scheme sets price at its prestabilization mean, the general result is that consumers lose and producers gain if the disturbance arose from production and vice versa if the disturbance arose from consumption, confirming the Waugh-Oi-Massell results (Gilbert, 1986). However, in general, stabilization of a quantity-shifting disturbance at its means will change mean price. (An exception is the special case in which supply and demand are linear and the disturbance is additive as in the Waugh-Oi-Massell analyses.) When the analysis is generalized to include lagged production and rational expectations, the distributional results depend not only on the location of the disturbance (in production or demand) but also on the elasticity of supply response and both the elasticity and curvature of demand, i.e., elasticity of marginal revenue (see Wright, 1979, and Newbery and Stiglitz, 1979).

If the above comparative statics approach were the appropriate analysis for proposed changes in storage policy, the results would be somewhat discouraging, apart from one fairly general finding relevant to agriculture--that stabilization of a regional production disturbance would generally reduce steady-state expected producer surplus in other unaffected regions (or countries). Other results depend (for their signs, not just their magnitudes) on parameters--in particular, consumption demand curvature--that are difficult to estimate and about which we have little information.

But the steady-state results do not tell us what happens to producers or consumers when price-support policy is changed in a world where intertemporal links in competitive production and storage exist and where productive assets are durable. In this more realistic world, changes in current supplies change the expected stream of profits from future production. This change in the expected stream will be capitalized as changes in the value of fixed or quasi-fixed productive assets.

To illustrate these dynamic effects, I will use a model described in detail in Wright and Williams (1986a). Consumption demand elasticity is constant at 0.2, storage (public or private) has constant marginal cost of 2.5 percent of the price at which consumption equals mean production, the interest rate is 5 percent per year, and supply elasticity is zero. The disturbance is a symmetric, independently and identically distributed, multiplicative shift of supply.[2] Private agents have rational expectations, and private storers are modeled as risk-neutral expected profit maximizers.

Consider the case illustrated by the solid line in Figure 1 where production is random and an unusually large amount (120 percent of mean production) is available from harvest and carry-in storage. For convenience, we assume this entire available supply is sold in year 0 to consumers or holders of carry-out stocks. Given inelastic demand, the large amount on hand will lower initial revenue from sales to stockholders and consumers below its steady-state mean R_{ss} to R_0. Profit-maximizing storage arbitrage increases the carryover beyond its mean steady-state level. Price expected in the second period is higher than current price (P_0) by the marginal carrying cost of stocks but below the steady-state mean (P_{ss}). The return R_1 to the year 1 harvest, expected as of year 0, $E_0[R_1]$, is even lower than R_0 because in this example the decrease in the expected volume of production to its mean outweighs the increase in market price.[3] In any later period t, the expected revenue, $E_0[R_1]$, depends on the price realizations at each harvest realization. The lower near-term prices induce higher

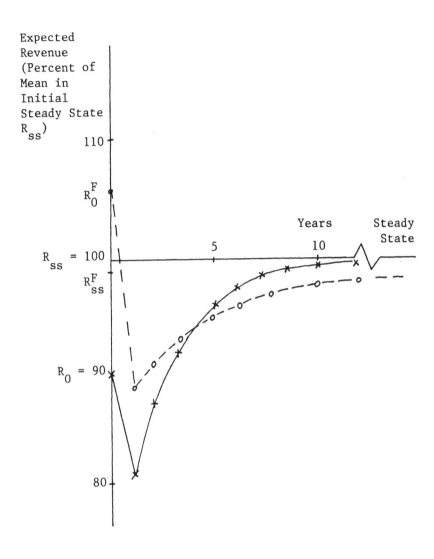

FIGURE 1.   The Expected Path of Revenue and the Effect of
Year 0 Introduction of a Price Floor (Case with High
Initial Available Supply)

consumption, causing expected stocks, $E_0[S_t]$, to decline monotonically to their steady-state level as t increases; this in turn causes the expected price, $E_0[P_t]$, to rise toward its steady-state mean. By t = 3, expected revenue, $E_0[R_3]$, is above R_0 but still well below R_{ss}.

What happens in this case if a price floor greater than P_0 is announced and introduced at year 0? The effect of a permanent price floor P^F equal to 90 percent of the price at mean output is shown by the dashed path in Figure 1.

In year 0, revenue (the value of initial available supplies) is higher than R_{ss} because the deviation of the price floor from Pss is less than the deviation of initial available supply Ao from its steady-state value A_{ss}. The higher price in year 0 due to the price floor reduces consumption and increases carryover to year 1; but the price floor cushions the effect on expected revenue, raising it above the free-market (solid curve) level for year 1.

But the price floor tends to increase expected carryover and reduce the rate of sell-off of excess stocks. In addition, the stabilization of consumption--in this example with constant demand elasticity of -0.2--causes the new steady-state revenue, R_{ss}^F, to be less than R_{ss}, consistent with previous comparative static results for stabilization with this demand specification (Wright, 1979 and Newbery and Stiglitz, 1979) as shown on the right-hand side of the diagram. The combined effects of expected slower sell-off of excess carryover and lower R_{ss}^F mean that $E_0[R_t]$ is reduced by the price floor for $t \geq 4$. (If demand were instead linear in the same example, the steady-state effect would be positive as predicted by comparative statics results, but the slower sell-off associated with the price floor would cause the expected revenue path to fall below the free-market path for intermediate values of t, then cross back as the (slower) expected sell-off neared completion.)

The vertical difference between the path of expected producer revenues is plotted in Figure 2. In this example with no supply elasticity, revenues equal annual profits. The immediate effects on profits are highly positive, but they decrease over time--a qualitative pattern invariant to many changes in specification, given high initial available supplies, as shown in Wright and Williams (1986a).[4] After some time has elapsed, revenues may well be below what they would have been without the price floor.

One might be tempted to conclude from these results that introduction of a price floor makes producers better

38

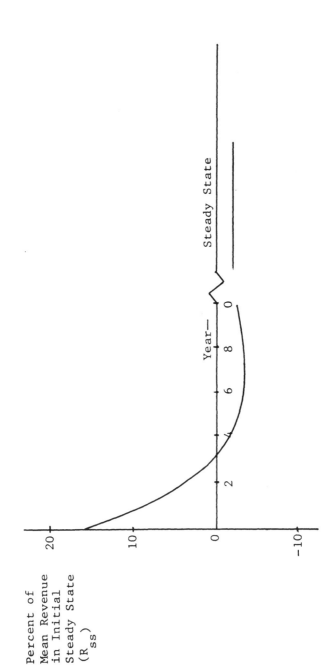

FIGURE 2. Expected Effect of Year 0 Introduction of a Floor Price Scheme on the Revenue Path (Case with High Initial Available Supply)

off in the short run but worse off in the medium run. In general, however, such a conclusion is incorrect. Assuming the existence of a capital market, the change in expected future revenue paths will be capitalized in fixed production assets (aggregated as "land" here). The change in land value equals the change in the present value of revenue discounted at appropriate interperiod interest rates, allowing for market risk premia if necessary. Upon announcement, the values of commodity stocks and land jump discontinuously. Current (year 0) owners have one-time gains or losses. Later purchasers trade at the new asset prices and neither gain or lose (in expectation), from the year 0 policy change, despite its effect on the expected path of revenue and its stability.[5]

How do current producers (holders of productive assets) fare? For a given path, the answer obviously depends on the discount rate between periods and who pays for the scheme. In this example, shown as Case I in Figure 3, the fall in land values (calculated net of the cost of the scheme) slightly outweighs the boost in value of the initial available supplies when $P^F = 90$. Higher price floors (e.g., $P^F = 95$) increase the initial revenue boost, causing the net values of land and stocks to increase. Thus, even if the costs of the scheme are raised by lump-sum taxes on producers (e.g., land taxes), the inference from the steady-state response for this case with constant and low demand elasticity is reversed.

Does such a scheme make sense as a means of wealth transfer? The answer depends on, among other things, the location of the market disturbance (in demand or supply) and the relative weights placed on consumers and year 0 producers. Figure 3 shows the effects of various price floors on year 0 producers for four cases. As noted above, a sufficiently high floor ($P^F = 95$) is more beneficial to producers than a lower floor. Linear demand (Case II) makes a price floor more favorable to producers than a convex demand, such as the constant elasticity case. But if the disturbance is in demand (rather than supply), year 0 producers gain much less from the introduction of a floor price; in the case of constant demand elasticity (Case III), they lose even at the highest floor shown--95 percent of the price at mean production.

Based on numerical examination of many variations in the parameters of this model (Wright and Williams, 1986a), we can make the following generalization is possible. Introduction of a given low price floor may increase or

40

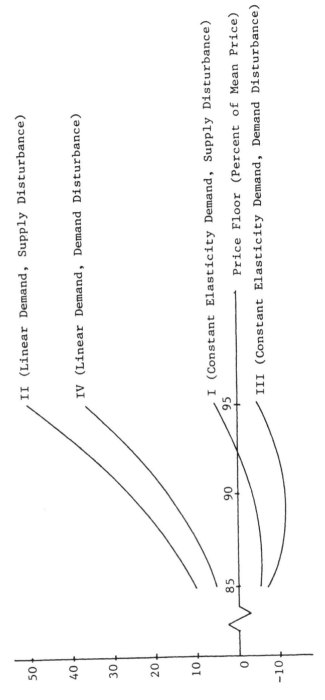

FIGURE 3. Effect of Introduction of a Price Floor on Wealth of Year 0 Producers
(High Initial Available Supply)

decrease the wealth of year 0 producers net of program costs, but introduction of a sufficiently higher price floor (below the new steady-state mean price) will increase asset values relative to the effect of the low price floor. Producers should not want the scheme to be an occasional "disaster prevention"; rather, if they want such a scheme at all, they want a high floor with frequent intervention and high mean stock levels.

Whether any of these schemes shown in Figure 3 is desirable depends on the weight placed upon expected consumer welfare. If consumers have zero weight (perhaps the case if they are foreigners), then a high price floor (e.g., P^F = 95) is desirable in Cases I, II, and III listed in Figure 3 relative to no intervention. Introduction of a high price floor (P^F = 95) is a profitable means of exploiting the low demand elasticity of consumers during the early stock accumulation phase--without changing expected steady-state consumption at all--in the case of zero supply response.

In the context of this model, other schemes to exploit consumers may be more profitable. Even if mean steady-state consumption is preserved, one expects that a more complex storage intervention might be more effective. But in practice, it is plausible that the cost of extra sophistication in terms of operation and control might outweigh any benefits. Of course, the existence of inelastic demand implies that acreage diversion or other schemes of production control can be more efficient means of extracting transfers from consumers than any floor price scheme. Acreage diversions have been a major part of U.S. farm policy. Why are they not made even more severe? And why would the government use storage-based price supports as well?

These questions lead the discussion away from the model and into the thickets of speculative political economy. The following are some hypotheses for consideration:

1. Even if the welfare of consumers, domestic or foreign, is not part of the public objective function, consumer attitudes may be a constraint on transfer policy. Schemes such as acreage diversions that reduce expected output are fairly obviously contrary to consumer interests unless they can be presented as having some plausible benefits, such as reducing a large costly government stockpile. (If all storage were in private hands, consumer attitudes might be much less sympathetic.) Hence, a storage scheme might be needed

to transform an output control scheme into a more acceptable public stockpile control scheme.

2. The storage-based price floor schemes are obviously not designed for long-run exploitation. They have little effect on expected steady-state consumption, assuming as we do here that the floor is not set so high as to rule out attainment of a stochastic steady state. There is no effect if supply elasticity is zero, and very little effect (of ambiguous sign) in reasonable cases if supply is more responsive (Wright and Williams, 1986a). Consumers and foreign importers might see the introduction of the scheme as prudent and stabilizing accumulation when supplies are cheap rather than as a scheme to exploit them by reducing their consumption in the short run. Indeed, the United States occasionally has been described as bearing the burden of providing food security for the world via its own stockpiling.

3. Thus far, the discussion has concentrated on the effects on producers. But in general, the effects on consumers, especially domestic consumers, must have at least some relevance for policy. Since rights to consumption are held by all consumers present and future (subject only to their budget constraints), anticipated consumer benefits of the introduction of a price floor scheme are not all capitalized as changes in asset values of current (year 0) consumers. Future consumers, unlike future entrants into production, can also suffer gains and losses from current policy changes. It might be argued that one benefit of price floor schemes is stabilization of consumption of risk-averse consumers. In developed countries such as the United States, comparative statics analysis indicates that where agricultural products have a small budget share, mean-preserving consumption stabilization is not necessarily desired by consumers even if they are risk averse with respect to income and all other prices are stable (Wright and Williams, 1986b). In the model considered above, if consumers prefer consumption stabilization in the steady state, as they do in Cases I and III, then year 0 producers tend to gain less from the introduction of a price floor scheme, though along the dynamic path to the steady state, they gain and consumers lose in the near term from the higher prices under a floor price scheme.

Given the constraints on alternative transfer mechanisms, it may be that introduction of a floor price scheme is the most efficient transfer mechanism under appropriate market conditions. If the deadweight loss is calculated assuming equal weight for consumers and producers, the deadweight loss of the transfer at $P^F = 95$ is about one-fifth of the next wealth increase for Case II above, and over one-half for Case I.[6] These deadweight loss proportions are not at all outrageous relative to the (very wide) range currently discussed in the public finance literature (see, for example, Browning, 1987). In the cases discussed here, however, the costs of the schemes are assumed to be paid for by a lump-sum producer levy. The marginal welfare cost associated with more usual means of taxation, which is the focus of the public finance literature, might greatly increase to the total welfare cost of the transfer. The relationship is not additive in general; a full analysis with distortionary taxes is beyond the scope of this study.

These deadweight loss figures assume very low world-demand elasticity. It is important to note the efficiency of price supports declines as the demand elasticity increases. As exports have become a more important market for U.S. agriculture in recent years, one might expect that the overall demand would have become more elastic and that demand fluctuations (mainly attributable to supply disturbances in foreign markets and to abrupt changes in policy in centralized economies) would have become more important relative to supply disturbances. If these conjectures are correct, then storage-based price supports are less efficient transfer mechanisms now than previously in the United States. Thus, the current tendency of U.S. policy to move away from reliance on storage schemes for transfers to producers is consistent with the increased importance of foreign markets. At the same time, higher demand elasticity reduces the expense associated with the disposal of accumulated stocks associated with the transition to a more market-oriented regime with "decoupled" transfers. We appear to be observing this transition now in the move to greater reliance on target prices less closely tied to output as a means of transfer to producers.

But the overall demand elasticity, taking foreign competitive responses into account, obviously still is quite low. As the United States tries to buy its farmers out of the later stages of the floor price cycle (high stocks, low revenues), its actions are expensive domestically and highly disruptive internationally in the short run.

INTERACTIONS BETWEEN NATIONAL POLICIES IN WORLD MARKET
STABILIZATION

A discussion of U.S. storage-based market stabilization
policy must recognize the strong interactions between
domestic policy and the policies of foreign exporters and
importers. As noted above, the level of storage needed to
achieve a given degree of price stabilization, taking
policies of other nations as given, is strongly dependent on
the export demand elasticity. There is broad agreement that
the export demand elasticity for major crops is not nearly
as high as it would be if there were no direct or indirect
trade barriers in the world market. Many countries manage
trade to stabilize consumer prices, thereby preventing their
consumers and producers from contributing to world market
stabilization. These policies are less costly to such
countries when the excess supply that they face is made more
elastic by a price floor scheme in the United States.

In this sense then, a storage-based floor price scheme
encourages importer policies that limit U.S. export market
expansion and tend to make world price less stable. Shei
and Thompson (1977) and Bale and Lutz (1981) show the
negative effects of trade barriers on market stability. The
corollary is that in a free world market the storage needed
to achieve any degree of price stability is much lower than
in a market with trade restrictions (Johnson and Sumner,
1976). Trade liberalization is highly effective in
stabilizing the world market price; this does not mean, of
course, that it necessarily stabilizes producer income flows
(see above and Newbery and Stiglitz, 1981, chapter 23; and
1984).

In a recent empirical study, Tyers and Anderson (1986)
estimate the effects of various degrees of liberalization on
the world market for several commodities. For wheat, the
coefficient of variation of price falls from 0.45 to 0.10
with global market liberalization, while solely industrial-
country or solely developing-country liberalizations yield
coefficients of variation of 0.31 or 0.23, respectively.
For coarse grains, the coefficient of variation falls from
0.19 to 0.08 with full liberalization. Solely developed- or
developing-country liberalizations are less effective,
yielding figures of 0.17 or 0.14, respectively. These
results raise the interesting paradox that abandonment of
storage-based price supports in the United States might
actually stabilize the world market price (and the domestic
price) in the long run if it encourages liberalization of
trade policies of other countries. This result would be in

direct contrast to the effects of U.S. policy taking
foreign policies as given. (See Rausser and Wright, 1987,
for a discussion of the role of export pricing in
negotiating multilateral trade liberalization).

CONCLUSIONS

Though storage-based price-support schemes (such as
nonrecourse loans and the farmer-owned reserve) have clearly
been important in past U.S. policy cycles, the size of
public and publicly-controlled stocks overstates their
effect because of substantial substitution for free private
stocks (Wright, 1985). Furthermore, these schemes are, from
the producer viewpoint, principally instruments of
redistribution rather than stabilization. This is true even
if, as assumed here, the support price is below the mean
free-market steady-state price. Given other hedging
options, the effects of stabilization schemes on allocative
efficiency of producers are likely to be too small to
justify their existence on efficiency grounds.

In determining redistribution, the dynamics of
adjustment to policy changes tend to increase the gains to
producers at the expense of consumers, beyond the
redistribution implied by comparative statics analysis. But
the gains (or possibly losses) are capitalized so that the
only producers who benefit are those who own fixed or
quasi-fixed production assets at the time when policy
changes become known. The prospects of future entrants
to farming (unless they receive bequests from current asset
owners) are not substantially affected.

Because consumption benefits are not capitalized,
future consumers are affected by current stabilization
policies, but the effect depends on parameters that are
difficult to quantify. In the short run, consumers are
negatively affected by the initial increase in storage
demand.

The assumption that the policy of other nations is
exogenous is important and may be invalid. Domestic
stabilization schemes tend to favor foreign nations
(especially the Eastern Bloc) that insulate their consumers
from market shocks. It is conceivable, then, that the
current trend towards removal of price supports, if
maintained in the long run, could encourage liberalization
of foreign markets, thereby increasing the natural
stabilizing role of the international marketplace and
reducing the size of domestic stocks.

NOTES

1. Here modification includes introduction of another disturbance negatively correlated with the original disturbance, as in the "two regions" example of Newbery and Stiglitz (1981, chapter 23).

2. The disturbance has a symmetric five-point distribution with values of -15 percent, -7.5 percent, 0, 7.5 percent, and 15 percent, with probabilities 0.05, 0.20, 0.50, 0.20, and 0.05, respectively.

3. The values, R_t, $t > 0$, are generated as the means for the tth period of a sample of 10,000 simulated runs of the numerical model with profit-maximizing private storage and random production, each starting with the same initial availability equal to 120 percent of mean production.

4. If initial available supplies are below the steady-state mean, the path of expected revenue changes starts at zero, rises and then falls toward the steady state (see Wright and Williams, 1986a).

5. If some future purchasers have risk preferences markedly different from those of all other producers, and markets are incomplete, they may gain or lose from changes in the riskiness of the revenue stream. This conjecture is not likely to invalidate the broad thrust of the conclusion presented here.

6. Cases III and IV, with disturbance in demand, exhibit much higher deadweight losses if the source of disturbance is supply fluctuations by foreign competitors whose welfare is not included in the model (see Wright and Williams, 1986a).

REFERENCES

Bale, Malcolm D. and Ernst Lutz. "Price Distortions in Agriculture and Their Effects: An International Comparison." _American Journal of Agricultural Economics_ 63(1981):8-22.

Browning, E.K. "On the Marginal Welfare Cost of Taxation." _American Economic Review_ 77(1987):11-23.

Council of Economic Advisors. _Economic Report of the President_. Washington, D.C.: GPO, 1986 and 1987.

Gilbert, Christopher L. "Commodity Price Stabilization: The Massell Model and Multiplicative Disturbances." _Quarterly Journal of Economics_ 101(1986):635-640.

Gustafson, Robert L. <u>Carryover Levels for Grain: A Method For Determining Amounts That Are Optimal Under Specified Conditions</u>. Washington, D.C.: U.S. Department of Agriculture, Technical Bulletin 1178, 1958a.

----------. "Implications of Recent Research on Optimal Storage Rules." <u>Journal of Farm Economics</u> 40(1958b):290-300.

Johnson, D. Gale and Daniel Sumner. "An Optimization Approach to Grain Reserves for Developing Countries." <u>Analysis of Grain Reserves: A Proceedings</u>. Washington, D.C.: U.S. Department of Agriculture, Economic Research Service, in cooperation with the National Science Foundation, ERS Report No. 634, August, 1976, pp. 56-76.

Massell, Benton F. "Price Stabilization and Welfare." <u>Quarterly Journal of Economics</u> 83(1969):284-298.

Newbery, David M.G. "Commodity Price Stabilization in Imperfect or Cartelized Markets." <u>Econometrica</u> 52(1984):563-578.

Newbery, D.M.G. and J.E. Stiglitz. "The Theory of Commodity Price Stabilization Rules: Welfare Impacts and Supply Responses." <u>Economic Journal</u> 89(1979):799-817.

----------. <u>The Theory of Commodity Price Stabilization</u>. Oxford: Clarendon Press, 1981.

----------. "Pareto Inferior Trade." <u>Review of Economic Studies</u> 51(1984):1-12.

Oi, W.Y. "The Desirability of Price Instability Under Perfect Competitions." <u>Econometrica</u> 27(1961):58-64.

Paul, Allen B. "The Pricing of Binspace: A Contribution to the Theory of Storage." <u>American Journal of Agricultural Economics</u> 52(1970):1-12.

Rausser, Gordon C. and Brian D. Wright. "Alternative Strategies for Trade Policy Reform." Working Paper No. 441, Department of Agricultural and Resource Economics, University of California, Berkeley, CA, 1987.

Samuelson, Paul A. "Stochastic Speculative Price." <u>Applied Mathematical Sciences</u> 68(1971):894-896.

Scheinkman, Jose A. and Jack Schechtman. "A Simple Competitive Model with Production and Storage." <u>Review of Economic Studies</u> 50(1983):417-441.

Schmitz, Andrew. <u>Commodity Price Stabilization: The Theory and Its Application</u>. Washington, D.C.: World Bank, Staff Working Paper No. 668, 1984.

48

Shei, Shun-Yi and Robert L. Thompson. "The Impact of Trade Restrictions on Price Stability in the World Wheat Market." _American Journal of Agricultural Economics_ 59(1977):628-638.

Turnovsky, S.J. "The Distribution of Welfare Gains From Price Stabilization: The Case of Multiplicative Disturbances." _International Economic Review_ 17(1976):133-148.

Tyers, Rodney, and Kym Anderson. "Distortions in World Food Markets: A Quantitative Assessment." Background Paper for the _1986 World Development Report_. Washington, D.C.: World Bank, 1986.

Waugh, Frederick V. "Does the Consumer Benefit from Price Instability?" _Quarterly Journal of Economics_ 58(1944):602-614.

Williams, Jeffrey C. _The Economic Function of Futures Markets_. Cambridge, England: Cambridge University Press, 1986.

Wright, Brian D. "The Effects of Ideal Production Stabilization: A Welfare Analysis Under Rational Behavior." _Journal of Political Economy_ 87(1979):1011-1033.

----------. "Commodity Market Stabilization in Farm Programs." In _U.S. Agricultural Policies: The 1985 Farm Legislation_. Edited by Bruce L. Gardner. Washington, D.C.: American Enterprise Institute for Public Policy Research, 1985, pp. 257-282.

Wright, Brian D. and Jeffrey C. Williams. "The Economic Role of Commodity Storage." _Economic Journal_ 92(1982a):596-614.

----------. "The Roles of Public and Private Storage in Managing Oil Import Disruptions." _Bell Journal of Economics_ 13(1982b):341-353.

---------- "Anti-Hoarding Laws: A Stock Condemnation Reconsidered." _Journal of Agricultural Economics_ 66(1984a):447-455.

----------. "The Welfare Effects of the Introduction of Storage." _Quarterly Journal of Economics_ 99(1984b):169-182.

----------. "The Incidence of Market-Stabilizing Price Support Schemes." Unpublished manuscript, Brandeis University, Waltham, Massachusetts, 1986a.

----------. "Measurement of Consumer Gains from Market Stabilization." Mimeo, Brandeis University, Waltham, Massachusetts, 1986b.

----------. "'Convenience Yield' Elucidated." Mimeo,
    University of California, Department of Agricultural
    and Resource Economics, Berkeley, 1987.

Reaction

Walter N. Thurman

My reaction to Wright's paper and to the related work by Wright and Williams (1986 and 1984) is very favorable. Part of my admiration is methodological and part is substantive.

My admiration as to method stems from the fact that storage is hard to model. It is hard to model because of an infinite regress problem. One would like to know how the storage decisions of private speculators depend upon today's price. All else equal, an increase in today's price makes selling today more attractive and storing for sale tomorrow less attractive. All else is not equal, however. At least it is difficult to know what to impound in ceteris paribus when determining the effect of current price on storage. After all, equilibrium in the market for storage equates today's price with the discounted expected future price: a higher current price will predict a higher future price.

How, then, does one think of the effect of today's price on private storage? Storage depends both upon today's price and upon the expectation of tomorrow's price, and the two are correlated. To form a price expectation for tomorrow, one must look ahead to the market's determination of price tomorrow. But since tomorrow's price affects tomorrow's storage in the same way that today's price affects today's storage, it must be that to know (to forecast) tomorrow's price is to know (to forecast) tomorrow's expectation of the next period's price. To forecast the two-day-ahead price requires a forecast of the three-day-ahead price, and on into the infinite future.

Assistant Professor, Department of Economics and Business, North Carolina State University.

Thus, analysis of the dependence of private storage on current price requires analysis of all future prices. If there are other variables that affect current price (such as income which affects consumption demand), then the entire future of those variables also must be considered in constructing the storage function.

The infinite regress problem so far described is not unique to storage. Many macroeconomic models share this feature that the present depends upon expectations of all future periods. The rational expectations hypothesis is one way to close such a model--to solve for a closed form for (price) expectations and to derive the implied optimal decision rules. Wallis (1980) describes application of the rational expectations hypothesis to a structural model that is linear. There are many other techniques that can be used in analyzing dynamic linear models.

Unfortunately, these techniques do not apply directly to the storage problem as it is intrinsically nonlinear. The nonlinearity lies in the dependence of storage on price. It can be shown that storage will be decreasing in current price but must have a nonlinearity at the zero level of stocks, since stocks cannot be negative. If stocks are ever driven to zero, then further increases in consumption demand or decreases in supply must be met by price increases. In short, the nonnegativity constraint on stocks precludes closed-form solutions except in very special cases (e.g., Aiyagari, Eckstein, and Eichenbaum, 1980).

Wright and Williams (1986 and 1984) solve the infinite regress problem using the numerical methods of stochastic dynamic programming. It is related to the more recent work by Miranda and Helmberger (1986) on price bands and buffer stocks policies and, in macroeconomics, to the work by Labadie (1986) on asset pricing in nonlinear rational expectations models.

Wright presents a neat methodological attack on the storage modeling problem. His substantive contribution is important as well. Recognizing the existence of storage is important, as it implies adjustment paths to policy changes rather than instantaneous responses to such changes. Equivalently, storage spreads the effects of policy changes across periods. For example, profits adjust slowly to once-and-for-all changes in price support levels.

While adjustment in equilibrium profit flows is not instantaneous, asset prices will jump instantly to capitalize the future stream of gradual profit adjustments. If asset markets are efficient, then gradual adjustments in profits will not imply gradual adjustments in asset values. This implies that when commodity policy changes to the advantage or detriment of asset owners, it is only the current owners who bear the capital gain or loss. Future entrants into the commodity-producing industry pay for the effects of the policy change in the prices they pay for assets specialized in producing the commodity.

I have argued to this point that the Wright paper is useful in helping us think about the effects of policy changes. But is the model employed an empirical model? After all, the model does predict the effect on asset (say, land) prices of policy changes. Could those predictions be tested? The answer, I think, is no. The reason is that Wright's model analyzes adjustments to once-and-for-all, or permanent, changes in policy. In fact, once-and-for-all policy changes do not occur. Asset prices in real markets certainly depend upon expectations of future policy changes and not all policy changes are perceived as permanent. An empirical model would layer probability distributions for government policy on top of the distributions for prices found in Wright's model.

What would be the implications of such an empirical model of private storage and government price-support policy? Consider three possible versions. First, suppose that policy followed a random walk. Any policy changes would permanently change expectations of future policy, and the forecasts of all future price supports, for example, would equal the current support. The mean price path of adjustment to any single change in policy would be identical to that in Wright's model of once-and-for-all policy changes. Notice, however, that price uncertainty would increase relative to the certain policy case, a matter of no consequence to the risk-neutral inhabitants of Wright's model.

In a second version of the model, imagine that policy did not follow a random walk, but rather, followed a cycle. Wright introduces his analysis with some evidence that U.S. agricultural policy has followed roughly a ten-year cycle since World War II. Suppose that the policy cycle were deterministic. One could still carry through Wright's analysis and derive the price and profit adjustment paths to permanent changes in the cycle. I don't know what these paths would look like, but presumably they would have their own cyclic characteristics. They would certainly be more complicated than those paths adjusting to changes in constant policy paths. One lesson to be gleaned is that policy change makes policy analysis more difficult. This is

the essence of the Lucas (1976) critique: to analyze the
equilibrium adjustment to policy changes, one must
incorporate the market's expectations of future policy.

Third and finally, a certain type of policy
predictability would modify Wright's conclusion as to the
immediate capitalization of policy changes into asset
values. By definition, an efficient market will use all
available information in determining asset prices. But if a
policy is perceived as more permanent the longer it is
in place, then asset price adjustments to policy changes
will be gradual. It is as though policymakers must buy
belief in the permanence of their policy changes with
the passage of time. A policy that has been in place for
many years implies asset prices that will reflect the
continuance of that policy into perpetuity. This statement
assumes, of course, that there is not information to the
contrary from some source other than the policy
realizations.

Still, the general capitalization point stressed by
Wright remains. Asset values reflect expectations of profit
adjustment paths which, in turn, depend upon policy
expectations. Further, a continual stream of policy changes
induces a continual stream of capital gains and losses and
there are corresponding winners and losers. If one takes a
policy cycle view of the world, then this redistribution is
cyclic. This suggests an oscillating political equilibrium
in which first producers benefit and then consumers benefit.
Such an equilibrium is an intriguing and, to my knowledge,
unexplored hypothesis.

REFERENCES

Aiyagari, Sudhakar R., Zvi Eckstein, and Martin Eichenbaum.
    "Rational Expectations, Inventories and Price
    Fluctuations." Economic Growth Center Discussion Paper
    No. 363, Yale University, October 1980.
Labadie, Pamela. "Solving Nonlinear Rational
    Expectations Models for Estimation: An Application
    to an Asset Pricing Model with Currency." Paper
    presented at the summer meetings of the
    Econometric Society, Duke University, 1986.
Lucas, Robert E., Jr. "Econometric Policy Evaluation: A
    Critique." Journal of Monetary Economics
    1(1976):19-46.

Miranda, Mario J. and Peter G. Helmberger. "The Effects of Price Band Buffer Stock Programs." Agricultural Economics Staff Paper Series No. 256, University of Wisconsin-Madison, 1986.

Wallis, Kenneth F. "Econometric Implications of the Rational Expectations Hypothesis." _Econometrica_ 48(1980):49-73.

Wright, Brian D. and Jeffrey C. Williams. "The Welfare Effects of the Introduction of Storage." _Quarterly Journal of Economics_ 99(1984):169-182.

----------. "The Incidence of Market-Stabilizing Price Support Schemes." Unpublished manuscript, Brandeis University, Waltham, Massachusetts, 1986.

3

An Analysis of Alternative Market and Governmental Risk Transference Mechanisms

Paul L. Fackler

ABSTRACT

This paper contrasts several simple institutional structures that affect the risk environment faced by agricultural producers. Included is a base cash market case, futures and options market alternatives, and governmental price guarantee and crop insurance programs. In a situation in which both quantity and price are uncertain, each case produces a different pattern of revenues and costs. These differences lead to variations in the supply response to changes in the institutional structure, which in turn produces variations in the probabilities associated with alternate price/output combinations. The main point of this exercise is to point out that there is considerable variation in the incentive structure facing producers and that there is no substitute for the careful examination of these incentives in analyzing the impacts of alternate institutions, at both the individual and the market level.

INTRODUCTION

One of the current buzz words in agricultural policy analysis is "market orientation." The features of a market-oriented agriculture are not completely clear, and many (often conflicting) policies vie for this title. This new orientation has led to an examination of market institutions that share similar functions with governmental programs, with agricultural futures and options on futures receiving particular attention. Indeed, the latter have a number of features in common with governmental price support programs. The suggestion has been made that the opening of option

Assistant Professor, North Carolina State University.

markets provides a way by which the government can reduce
its role in commodity markets and shift its burden onto the
free market.

While it is certainly true that futures and options
markets share some of the characteristics of government
price stabilization and support programs, there are a number
of fundamental differences between these institutions. To
formulate useful policies it is important that the
similarities and differences be recognized and accounted
for. These institutions resemble one another in that they
can facilitate the transfer of risk between various economic
groups. On the other hand, the nature of the risk
transferred and the cost to various groups differ
substantially. Consequently, the nature of the output and
price changes as well as distributional changes will
differ depending on the exact nature of the alternative
considered.

In this paper, some aspects of these relationships will
be explored by examining incentives that individual
agricultural producers have to participate in futures,
options, and various governmental risk transfer programs.
Particular mention shall be made of price guarantees, with
and without acreage or production restrictions or
allotments, and crop insurance. The focus will be on
describing in simple terms differences in revenues and
costs associated with several alternatives. Some comments
also will be made on the problem of modeling the induced
supply effects resulting from introduction of a program or a
market.

In what follows, the revenue recieved by an individual
producer, given the use of a particular risk transference
mechanism, will be examined. This revenue is conditional
on the levels of production and the prices received, both of
which are taken to be random. This examination points out
some significant differences in the incentives producers
face, given alternate institutional arrangements. Cost
aspects also are important, and analysis of the incidence of
these costs is necessary to assess the likely level of
producer participation and the consequent supply response.
Following this is a discussion of some of the problems
arising in analysis of the aggregate impacts of these
arrangements on output and price patterns. A concluding
section completes the paper.

REVENUE EFFECTS OF ALTERNATE RISK TRANSFERENCE INSTITUTIONS

In this section, the revenue positions of various simple institutions for transferring risk shall be compared. These comparisons apply to the situation faced by producers of seasonal crops, who face two types of risk: quantity (or yield) risk and price risk. In the absence of any governmental programs or forward-pricing mechanisms, revenues from the sale of a crop at harvest will be equal to the quantity produced times the harvest-time market price (denoted R=QP).[1] Prior to harvest, neither Q nor P is known with certainty, and hence R also will be random. The different price-quantity combinations necessary to produce given levels of revenues are illustrated in Figure 1: Cash Market. Notice that an increase in either P or Q will always result in an increase in R as well.

Suppose a producer is able to trade in a futures market. A short position in futures essentially commits the producer to sell a given amount (s) at the current futures price (f). Revenues therefore will equal the quantity produced less the short position times the market price plus the size of the short position times the futures price (R=(Q-s)P+sf).[2] In Figure 1: With Futures Contract, this situation is illustrated using f=1.5 and s=2. Notice that if the output actually turns out to be 2, the market price is irrelevant, as the producer will sell all of this output at 1.5. The prospects faced by this producer depend on whether the realized output is greater or less than 1.5 (Q>s or Q<s) and also on whether price is greater or less than 1.5 (P>f or P<f). If P<f then the producer is better off than in the cash market in the sense that more revenue is generated for any given level of output. If P>f the opposite is true. Notice that if Q>s, an increase in either P or Q leads to higher revenues, but if Q<s, an increase in P will lead to lower revenue (geometrically this is indicated by the concavity of the iso-revenue lines). Thus, a producer who enters a large short position actually may end up desiring the price to decrease. This seemingly perverse result occurs because when output cannot cover the futures position, the difference is essentially a short speculative position that benefits from a price decrease. In the face of output uncertainty, small futures positions may be appealing on the grounds that it will then be unlikely that realized output does not cover the futures position.

Options markets, which recently have been opened in a number of agricultural commodities, provide an alternative

60

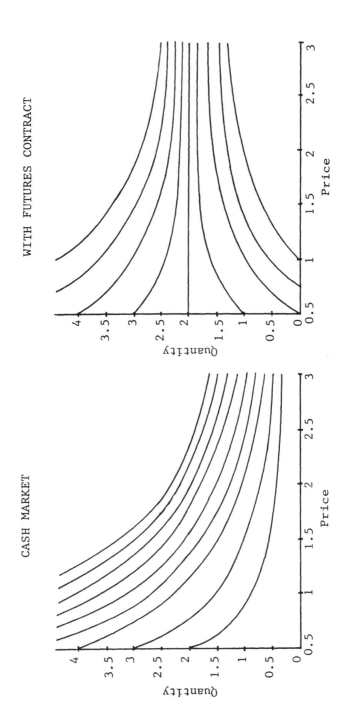

FIGURE 1. Iso-Revenue Lines for Alternative Scenarios

61

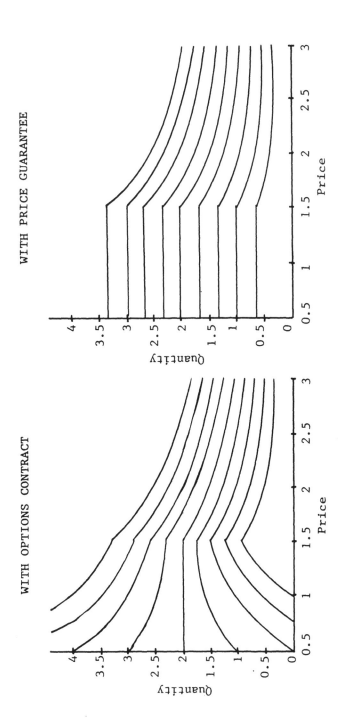

(FIGURE 1, continued)

62

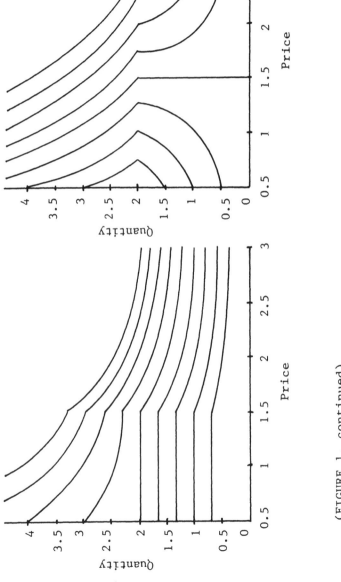

(FIGURE 1, continued)

market tool with which a producer transfers risk. Examined
here is a strategy involving buying a put option. Such an
option gives the purchaser the right to sell an amount (o)
of a commodity at a specified exercise price (x) on or
before a given date. If the market price is above the
exercise price (P>x), the purchaser can simply ignore
the option and sell the product at the higher price. Thus,
an options contract essentially provides a price floor on a
fixed amount of the product. The revenues from such a
strategy are R=QP if P>x and R=(Q-o)P+ox if P<x. In
Figure 1: With Options Contract, this situation is
illustrated with o=2 and x=1.5. Notice that for P>x, this
situation is the same as the cash market case, whereas for
P<x, it is identical to the futures market case, with f=x
and s=o. Thus, an options position yields revenues that are
always at least as great as those obtained in the cash
market or through futures alternatives. Furthermore, the
most objectionable feature of the futures strategy, the
situation in which P>f and Q<s and a producer loses from a
price increase and is worse off than in the base case, is
eliminated with an options position. There remains,
however, the feature that a price decrease is desirable
when P<x and Q<o.

Of the governmental programs designed to alter the risk
environment faced by agricultural producers, the first to be
considered is a price guarantee on all output. Such a
program could be accomplished through governmental purchases
or through direct payments to producers; or, if the good
were traded, through either export subsidies or import
restrictions, depending on whether there were a net excess
supply or demand for the good. Regardless of what method is
used to implement the program, a given price/quantity
combination will yield identical revenues of R=QP if P>m and
R=Qm if P<m, where m is the guaranteed minimum price. As
illustrated in Figure 1: With Price Guarantee, where m=1.5,
this makes revenue independent of the market price as long
as that price is below the minimum. This type of program is
similar to the current soybean loan program (though there
are acreage reductions tied to program participation, these
affect the level of output, not the revenue given that
output level).

It is sometimes argued that a price guarantee program
is like the provision of a put option with an exercise price
equal to the guaranteed minimum price. A comparison of the
iso-revenue lines for these two cases reveals that this is
somewhat misleading when output is not known with certainty.
There are two reasons for differences in the revenue derived

from these alternatives. First, the price guarantee applies to all output, while the option applies to a fixed amount of output. This means that any excess output beyond that hedged by the option will be sold at the market rate, resulting in lower profit than that realized under the price guarantee program. The second reason is that when there is an output shortfall with an options position (Q<o), the producer essentially is acting as a speculator. This means that a low price/low output situation provides additional revenue from the speculative part of the options position. Parenthetically, Marcus and Modest (1986) recently demonstrated that minimum price guarantees can be thought of as a random number of put options and develop a formula for determining the ex ante value of such a program.[3]

An alternative price guarantee program would be one that covers only a fixed amount of production (an allotment or quota). This would eliminate the first of the differences between a price guarantee and an options position discussed above. With such a program, if production falls below the allotment, then all output is priced at the guaranteed price. However, if output is greater than the allotment, the excess production is priced at the market price. Thus $R=QP$ when $P>m$, but when $P<m$, revenues will depend on whether realized output is greater or less than the production allotment (a): $R=Qm$ if $Q<a$ and $R=(Q-a)P+am$ if $Q<a$. Such a program is similar to the current peanut program and the iso-revenue lines associated with it are illustrated in Figure 1: With Price Guarantee on Allotment. Notice that this program still differs from the options case in that a low price/low output situation results in less revenue than in the case with options.

A final program to consider is a crop insurance program. The current program has the following features. A producer can elect a certain yield coverage and price. If yield, and therefore output, fall below the insured level, the producer receives a payment equal to the output shortfall times the elected price. Actual output is sold at the going market price. Thus, $R=QP$ if $Q>i$ and $R=QP+(i-Q)e$ if $Q<i$, where i is the insured output level and e is the elected price. In Figure 1: With Crop Insurance, the iso-revenue lines are depicted for the case in which $i=2$ and $e=1.5$. The notable feature in this figure is the backward-bending lines when $P<e$ and $Q<i$. This indicates that in the low price/low output situation, for a given realized price, the producer is better off with less output, since any output produced receives a lower price than that obtained on the insured output shortfall.

The revenue formulas for each of the six alternatives examined here are summarized in Table 1. A few points are worth mentioning in relation to this table. First, a number of the alternatives are alike in certain regions of the price/quantity plane. For example, the options, and both price guarantee alternatives match the cash market alternatives when price is greater than the exercise/ guarantee price. The options alternative matches that of the futures when price is below the exercise/futures price, whereas it matches that of the price guarantee on an allotment when either price is above the exercise/minimum price or when output is above the hedge level/allotment. With the crop insurance alternative, when quantity is above the insured level, the cash market case is matched.

Another method of contrasting these alternative marketing arrangements is to examine each of their effective prices. The effective price is defined as that price which, when multiplied by the realized output, equals the actual realized revenue, i.e., $P^*Q=R$ or $P^*=R/Q$, where P^* denotes the effective price. The formulas for deriving these are also given in Table 1 for each of the alternatives. Two points are worth noting concerning these effective prices. First, except in the futures case, the effective price is always at least as great as the realized price. This fact may be verified by checking the signs of any of the amounts added to the realized price to derive the effective price. In the futures case, this amount will be negative when $P>f$; this may be one implicit reason why agricultural producers have not become heavily involved in futures markets.

The second point concerns which alternatives would be preferred on the basis of revenue. To make such comparisons, it is assumed that, where appropriate, the alternatives have comparable output and price "guarantee" levels, i.e., $s=o=a=i$ and $f=x=m=e$. When costs are ignored, a dominance relationship occurs if the effective price for one alternative is always higher than that for another. Thus, the cash market alternative is dominated by all the other alternatives except that for the futures, and the futures alternative is dominated by the options alternative. The options alternative also dominates the minimum price guarantee on an allotment alternative, as does the simple price guarantee alternative. This assertion results from the fact that $m \gtrless P+a(m-P)/Q$ when $a \gtrless Q$.

TABLE 1. Revenue and Effective Price Formulas for
Alternate Scenarios

Cash Market

$R = PQ \qquad\qquad P* = P$

With Futures Contract

$R = (Q-s)P + sf \qquad P* = P + \dfrac{s(f-P)}{Q}$

With Options Contract

$$R = \begin{cases} QP \\ (Q-o)P + ox \end{cases} \qquad P* = \begin{cases} P & P > x \\ P + \dfrac{o(x-P)}{Q} & P < x \end{cases}$$

With Price Guarantee

$$R = \begin{cases} QP \\ Qm \end{cases} \qquad P* = \begin{cases} P & P > m \\ m & P < m \end{cases}$$

With Price Guarantee on Allotment

$$R = \begin{cases} QP \\ Qm \\ (Q-a)P + am \end{cases} \qquad P* = \left.\begin{cases} P \\ m \\ P + \dfrac{a(m-P)}{Q} \end{cases}\right\} \begin{array}{l} \\ Q < a \\ Q > a \end{array} \left.\begin{array}{c} P > m \\ \\ P < m \end{array}\right\}$$

With Crop Insurance

$$R = \begin{cases} QP \\ QP + (i-Q)e \end{cases} \qquad P* = \begin{cases} P & Q > i \\ P + \dfrac{(i-Q)e}{Q} & Q < i \end{cases}$$

R = Revenue	o = short put option
P = Price	position
Q = Quantity	x = exercise price
P* = Effective Price	m = minimum guaranteed
(P*Q = R)	price
s = short futures position	a = production allotment
f = futures price	i = insured quantity
	e = elected insured price

COST CONSIDERATIONS

Thus far only producer revenue has been discussed. The alternatives also differ with respect to their costs, not only to producers but to taxpayers, consumers, and others. This section will briefly consider the direct costs, and some of the treasury implications of the various alternatives.

The cash market case, of course, involves no costs other than the amount paid by consumers to producers. Similarly, the futures case involves essentially no producer costs (strictly speaking, of course, there are brokerage and manager costs). For both the options and the crop insurance alternatives, a premium must be paid; this represents an increase in fixed production costs. The treasury costs in the crop insurance case equal $(i-Q)e$ less the premium paid if $Q<i$; if $Q>i$, the treasury gains the value of the premium. In any given year the treasury may be a net gainer or loser. In practice, crop insurance has not been a self-financing venture.

No treasury costs are incurred with the options alternative if the options are purchased in the market. There are problems, however, with a market-based program if this is taken to be a replacement for current commodity programs. First, it is possible that options sellers would demand a sizeable risk premium, making such an alternative quite expensive relative to the protection it provides. Second, the volume of option trading would have to increase by orders of magnitude from current levels to provide protection similar to that offered by current commodity programs.

Another way to implement an option-based alternative is for the government to offer options, with the program self-financing in the long run. In this case, the treasury costs would be $(x-P)o$ less the value of the premium if $P<x$. Again, the premium would represent a net treasury gain of $P>x$.

For both crop insurance- and government-sponsored option programs, the problem of premium setting arises. For crop insurance programs, in particular, the difficulties in setting premiums are exacerbated by problems of adverse selection and moral hazard. The first of these concepts refers to the participation in insurance schemes by those agents most likely to require settlements for incurred losses (see Skees and Reed, 1986). It is in the interests of those producers with lower mean yields to take advantage of crop insurance programs. Indeed, it is possible that some producers will find it advantageous to bring new land into production to take advantage of the insurance program. If premiums are based on average yields, then this self-selection process results in an insurance program that is not self-supporting. If premiums are raised as a result, this forces out the producers at the margin; these producers are either less risk averse or have higher average yields than do those that remain in the program. The adverse selection problem underscores the fact that insurance schemes typically subsidize inefficiency and penalize efficiency. The need to base premiums on producer performance has been a critical concern for the crop insurance program. Options programs are not plagued by the adverse selection problem since payments depend on the market price, which is the same for all producers.

The moral hazard problem also can arise with a crop insurance program. Moral hazard refers to differences in agents' behavior before and after obtaining insurance. Typically, when insured, agents have less incentive to guard against the insured risk, and therefore may increase the probability of its occurrence. This could lead agents to engage in riskier ventures such as use of crop varieties that have both higher expected and more variable yields.

In a sense, any increase in output resulting from programs associated with price risk can also be thought of as a moral hazard problem, since increased output increases the probability that any given payment will be required. Furthermore, the aggregate effects of an increase in output will result in price declines, increasing the probability that market price will fall below the insured level. This issue is explored more fully in the next section.

Simple price guarantee programs don't directly impose costs on producers. In practice, however, there are costs typically associated with program qualifications such as acreage restrictions. Furthermore, there are statutory payment limitations, though there seem to be myriad ways to avoid them. The treasury costs depend largely on how the program is implemented. If the program involves a simple direct payment, then the treasury cost equals $(m-P)Q$ if $P<m$ and zero otherwise (if the guarantee only covers an allotment, then the cost is $(m-P)a$ if $P<m$).

Another way of implementing the program is through purchase of enough of the commodity to maintain the price at the guarantee level. In this case the treasury cost will depend on the demand function $Q^d = Q^d(P)$; the cost will be $m(Q-Q^*)$ where $Q^* = Q^d(m)$ (see Figure 2). If the demand curve is inelastic in this range ($[Q^*,Q]$), then this arrangement

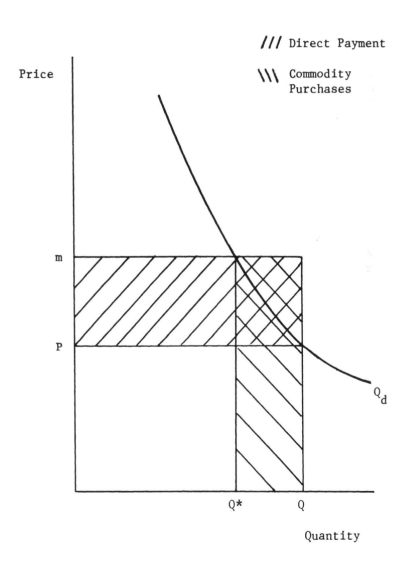

FIGURE 2.   Treasury Costs Associated with
Price Guarantee Programs

leads to lower treasury costs (since $mQ^* > PQ$). However, there could be substantial costs to consumers in the form of higher commodity prices. Export or other purchasing subsidies would entail the same costs as a direct payment to producers, import restrictions would impose costs on consumers similar to those under a purchase arrangement, while the treasury would gain revenues if tariffs were collected.

An additional problem with programs involving government purchase of excess supply, or indeed any program that sets the market price artificially high, is that additional investment is induced into the production of the commodity, both domestically and abroad. This can be viewed as a kind of free rider problem, with unintended "outside" investors benefiting from the "public good" nature of the program. This in turn necessitates increases in the size of the purchases necessary to maintain the guaranteed price, since the increased investment shifts outward the supply of the commodity.

In this country acreage restrictions tied to support price program participation have been used to help mitigate the oversupply problem. These restrictions, however, give rise to a kind of adverse selection problem. The restrictions have two major results. First, the worst land will be removed from production and second, the land remaining in production will tend to be farmed more intensively. The result is an increase in production greater than would be expected based on average yields times acres under cultivation. These factors must be accounted for in determining the output impact of price guarantees coupled with acreage restrictions.

OUTPUT AND PRICE CONSIDERATIONS

The previous sections have been concerned mainly with the revenues and costs associated with alternate scenarios for given price and quantity levels. These results are fairly easily obtained, and far more complex strategies can be similarly analyzed. The difficulty in evaluating alternative policies and institutions is that their implementation will alter the nature of the probabilities associated with alternate price/quantity combinations. Some of these problems already have been pointed out. These shifts come about for two reasons. First, producers face different profit possibilities for each scenario and consequently will have chosen different levels of production inputs. Second, when this effect is aggregated over many producers, there will be consequent changes in aggregate output, which will result in a shift in the price probability distribution. To the extent that producers anticipate such price distribution shifts, output probabilities will again be altered. Thus, there is a feedback loop in response to a shift in the risk/return environment. To assess the impact of such a shift, it is necessary to specify correctly the macro impacts of the micro responses of individual producers, who themselves are attempting to anticipate these same macro phenomena. The realization that such feedback loops occur has been the main impetus for the development of rational expectations and learning models, which attempt to arrive at equilibrium solutions to this feedback process.

In evaluating a program such as a price guarantee, it is sometimes assumed that such a program simply truncates the price distribution at the guaranteed price without effecting the upper portion of the distribution. This is an unrealistic assumption for the reasons given above. The further assumption that the expected price will remain unchanged (as, for example, in Petzel, 1984) is incompatible with the first assumption, since the expected price must increase if the first assumption is made. Similar comments can be made about a price guarantee on an allotment, which will not truncate the distribution but will shift probability mass away from the lower tail of the distribution.

Another distributional assumption that has appeared in the literature (Gallagher, 1978) has the price distribution truncated at the guarantee price, but with zero probability of the price being equal to the guarantee price, indicating that the program ensures that the price will be higher than the guarantee price. It would seem more reasonable to assume that the price distribution would be truncated at the guarantee price, with some positive probability of price being at this lower bound and with the probability distribution for higher values different from what it otherwise would have been. It should also be pointed out that truncation of the price distribution will depend on how the government actually carries out the program. If the price guarantee comes in the form of a direct payment, then the program will not truncate the market price distribution, though it will effect this distribution through the ensuing supply response. From a producer's point of view, however, and, therefore, for purposes of supply analysis, it is the distribution of the effective price that is important.

Similar remarks apply as well to market mechanisms for shifting risk. The question of the impact of futures markets on cash market prices long has been a subject of inquiry (e.g., Turnovsky, 1983). Options markets, on the other hand, typically are not thought to alter the distribution of prices on the commodities on which they are written. The reason this topic is rarely considered relates to the current state of option pricing theory. Virtually all of such theory relies on the ability to create a replicating portfolio, which involves holding a continuously readjusted amount of risk-free bonds and the underlying commodity. If a portfolio can be created that essentially mimics the behavior of the option, then the opening of an actual options market will not alter the prices of previously existing assets. There is, however, a Catch-22 in this reasoning, in that if such a replicating portfolio were actually possible, there would be no need to open the options market. Given that there is, in certain markets, a clear demand for options contracts, it is almost certain that these markets provide alternatives previously unavailable. This, in turn, will alter the risk/return situation faced by market participants and should, in general, lead to different price/quantity probabilities. Unfortunately, there currently is no way actually to test this theory in the United States, as the existence of governmental support programs precludes such an assessment.

To assess the impacts of alternative institutions adequately it would be desirable to have a model of producer behavior in a risky environment. The most widely used and accepted framework for such an analysis is the expected utility model. The basic features of such a model include the producer's utility function, U, which provides a representation of the producer's attitude toward risk, and the producer's subjective joint probability distribution for output and prices, $F(P,Q)$. The producer attempts to maximize the expected utility of profits (revenues minus costs) where the expectation is taken over prices or quantities.

Even this basic model, which is fairly simple, is complicated by the fact that the producer can, in theory, control the probability distribution of output as well as the correlation between farm level output and market price. A simple example of such control arises with the introduction of an irrigation system. This typically will raise average yield, reduce yield variability, and possibly lower the correlation between farm-level output and price. Indeed, when risk is introduced into the problem of firm-level decision making, there is a question of the meaning of price-taking behavior, since a producer can and should account for output/price correlation when making decisions. A reasonable extension of the price-taking concept to the risky environment is that the producer takes the marginal distribution of price as fixed, while having the ability to influence, within the limits of existing technologies, the moments of the quantity distribution as well as the cross moments of quantity and price.

Such a model can be quite difficult to work with and for present purposes an outline of a somewhat simpler model shall be proposed. Suppose that the producer can control only the amount of land, a, devoted to a given crop, with the yield, Y, on that land being a random variable with a fixed distribution. This simplifies the problem to one of determining the acreage response to the opening of a market or the introduction of a program.

Unfortunately, even this type of model provides analytical results only if some strong assumptions are made concerning the nature of the price/output distribution and the utility function. The study of Newbery and Stiglitz (1981), for example, perhaps the most exhaustive study of producer behavior in risky environments, uses a somewhat peculiar form of utility function to allow them derivation of analytical results. An alternative approach that sacrifices generality for the retention of the basic framework outlined above is outlined here as possibly a useful way to gain insight into the nature of supply responses.

The approach envisioned would involve simulation of producer response for some parametric forms for U and F. Given this initial information, the acreage level that maximizes expected utility could be calculated using numerical integration techniques. The problem is thus to maximize with respect to acreage, a, the function $E[U(R(a;P,Q)-C(a))]$, where R is one of the alternatives listed in Table 1 and C is the cost of production, a known function of acreage. This, in turn, would imply a new distribution for prices. Such price distributional changes would induce a second producer acreage response, and the maximization problem would have to be re-solved using the new price probability distribution. This process would be repeated in an iterative fashion until a stable price probability distribution is reached, presuming that such a stable solution exists. Such a modeling effort was not possible, given the deadline for delivery of this paper.

Such a simulation model, although capable of yielding insights, cannot yield information about the actual supply responses. Accurate econometric measurement of shifts in output and price probability distributions is a difficult problem and is complicated by a number of factors. First, current and historical situations do not fall neatly into simple scenarios. Futures markets exist for a number of major agricultural commodities and options markets recently have opened on some of these as well, including soybeans, corn, wheat, hogs and cattle. At the same time, the policy formation environment is in a continual state of flux, with program specifications changing yearly.

Furthermore, many programs have fairly complicated regulations concerning program qualification, maximum payments, calculation of the price used to determine payment size, and so forth. For example, a number of programs have a two-tiered price support structure. Thus, the peanut program has one price support for allotment peanuts and a lower support price for excess peanuts (additionals). The wheat and corn programs have target prices and lower loan prices. The relevant "market" prices used to implement the associated programs may not even be the same, with loan prices compared to actual prices available to producers and target prices related to a seasonal average price aggregated over a region. This is only one of the many problems related to data and choice of variables.

Another factor, neglected in this paper but important to account for in empirical studies, is the storage question, and, more generally, the dynamics of markets and policies. For many commodities storage dynamics will strongly affect the long-run outcome of government stabilization and support programs. For example, if a minimum price program is accomplished by government purchases, the stored crop at some point must be sold or given away (though it also could be dumped). When these stocks come on the market or displace market purchases, there will be a downward price response. This, of course, could, be part of a stabilization plan in which both low and high prices are avoided. The current loan program with its loan prices and release prices is intended, in theory, to operate in this fashion. There has been a tendency. however, to set loan rates and release prices too high to prevent continued accumulation of stocks. This, in turn, leads to the need for such measures as the PIK program to empty governmental storage bins.

The complications of real world programs lead to problems in specifying an appropriate empirical model for supply. Studies that have addressed this problem often attempt to construct effective prices for alternate uses of land, program participation, and marketing strategies (Gallagher, 1978). While this is a useful first step, the expected utility model outlined above suggests that the supply (acreage) response function has as an argument the entire joint probability distribution for price and outputs. Even if this distribution is parameterized in a relatively simple way, it is not at all clear how to incorporate this insight into an econometric framework. There is certainly room for further work in this area.

SUMMARY AND CONCLUSIONS

A number of mechanisms, both market and governmental, exist that alter the risk/return situation faced by agricultural producers. To assess the usefulness and the impact of these alternative mechanisms adequately, it is necessary first to clearly understand how such mechanisms alter the pattern of returns available to the producer. In a situation in which a producer faces both output and price risk, alternate mechanisms have significantly different returns for given output/price situations. That market mechanisms, particularly agricultural options, reproduce the random returns offered by governmental price guarantees and insurance programs is a belief that has been shown to be unfounded.

Examination of the patterns of producer returns, given alternate institutions, is only part of the analysis needed to measure the impact of such institutions. Also critical is an understanding of the shifts in output induced by such policies and the consequent changes in price distributions. A number of problems that complicate such an analysis have been discussed. The expected utility paradigm was briefly outlined, together with a simulation approach that might be useful in providing insight into the nature of price and output responses. Also mentioned were some of the problems involved in empirical analysis of institutional impacts on the commodity market. In particular, the changing institutional structure makes statistical modeling difficult.

The major point to emerge from this discussion is that alternate institutions must be analyzed carefully to assess their usefulness and impacts on agricultural producers, on consumers, and on taxpayers. While the current interest in moving toward a market-oriented agriculture may be well founded, it should not be assumed that a market mechanism will arise that can replicate the effects of government programs. Market mechanisms, in the long run, may indeed prove superior to governmental price guarantees and crop insurance, but reliance on them to mitigate the effects of risk on agricultural producers will change the nature of agriculture as it is presently practiced.

NOTES

1. Throughout the paper, random variables are denoted by capital letters, whereas known constants appear in lower case.

2. Basis considerations are ignored here but clearly introduce further risk in both futures and options markets.

3. After the conference, Bruce Gardner pointed out to me that current deficiency payment programs, in which payment is made on base output, are essentially identical to options controls.

REFERENCES

(References not explicitly referred to in the text are cited here as background.)

Chavas, Jean-Paul, Rulon D. Pope, and Robert S. Kao. "An Analysis of the Role of Futures Prices, Cash Prices and Government Programs in Acreage Response." Western Journal of Agricultural Economics 8(1983):27-33.

Gallagher, Paul. "The Effectiveness of Price Support Policy: Some Evidence for U.S. Corn Acreage Response." Agricultural Economics Research 30(1978):8-14.

Gardner, Bruce. "Commodity Options for Agriculture." American Journal of Agricultural Economics 59(1977):986-992.

Loehman, Edna, Michael S. Kaylen, and Paul V. Preckel. "Stochastic Microeconomic Production Modelling: Foundation for Policy Analysis Under Risk." In An Economic Analysis of Risk Management Strategies for Agricultural Production Firms, proceedings of a seminar sponsored by Southern Regional Project S-180, Tampa, FL, March 1986.

Marcus, Alan J. and David M. Modest. "The Valuation of a Random Number of Put Options: An Application to Agricultural Price Supports." Journal of Financial and Quantitative Analysis 21(1986):73-86.

Newbery, David M.G. and Joseph E. Stiglitz. The Theory of Commodity Price Stabilization. Oxford: Clarendon Press, 1981.

Petzel, Todd E. "Alternatives for Managing Agricultural Price Risk: Futures, Options, and Government Programs." AEI Occasional Paper. Washington, D.C.: American Enterprise Institute for Public Policy Research, 1984.

Pope, Rulon D. "Empirical Estimation and Use of Risk Preferences: An Appraisal of Estimation Methods That Use Actual Economic Decisions." American Journal of Agricultural Economics 64(1982):376-383.

Skees, Jerry R. and Michael R. Reed. "Rate Making for Farm-Level Crop Insurance: Implications for Adverse Selection." American Journal of Agricultural Economics 68(1986):653-659.

Turnovsky, Stephen J. "The Determination of Spot and Futures Prices with Storable Commodities." Econometrica 51(1983):1363-1387.

Reaction

Kandice H. Kahl

The paper by Paul Fackler represents useful research that will be particularly beneficial to those studying ways to make agricultural policy more market-oriented. Fackler combines many good ideas into the basis for an excellent paper. I have little disagreement with what he has done. These comments focus on major findings in the paper, possible extensions, areas that need clarification, and arguments that could be strengthened.

In the first section of the paper, Fackler reviews revenues under alternative marketing strategies, allowing both quantity and price to vary. In previous studies, marketing alternatives generally have been compared allowing only price to vary. When quantity risk is ignored, options and a price guarantee program give the same revenues. Thus, previous studies have concluded that options and a price guarantee program give similar results. Fackler demonstrates in this paper that when quantity risk is included, the revenues from options and a price guarantee program are not the same under all conditions. This finding is important for policy makers and is explained well in this paper.

Fackler compares the revenues from six marketing alternatives under various combinations of price and farm level output. In future research, one could determine the probabilities of the various price-output combinations. Instead of evaluating all price-output combinations equally, one could then focus more attention on those combinations that were more likely to occur.

Associate Professor, Department of Agricultural Economics and Rural Sociology, Clemson University.

Originally, when reviewing the Fackler analysis, I
thought that ignoring option premiums and crop insurance
premiums was a serious omission. I realize that premiums
are costs, and thus should not be included in revenues.
However, I questioned the idea of comparing gross revenues
rather than revenues net of significant costs incurred in
trading. Actually the inclusion of these costs would simply
amount to subtracting a constant (equal to the premium
multiplied by the quantity protected). Thus, the basic
implications would be the same.

I next questioned the omission of the basis. In the
graphs in the paper, the variable price represents either
the cash price or the futures price. One can use either
price because the two prices are assumed to be equal; that
is, the basis is assumed to be zero. Alternatively, one
could make the following two assumptions: (1) price
represents the cash price and (2) the basis can be predicted
perfectly. Under those conditions, the inclusion of the
basis would simply amount to adding a constant to revenues.
The constant would equal the quantity protected (i.e., the
quantity hedged in the futures or option market) multiplied
by the basis (which is assumed to be known). Of course, in
reality, the basis is a random variable and cannot be
predicted perfectly. Thus, the iso-revenue curves would not
be known with certainty. The inclusion of the basis,
however, would still give the same basic implications.

In the last part of the revenue section, Fackler shows
which marketing strategies dominate under some strict
assumptions. For example, he assumes that at-the-money put
options are purchased and that option premiums are ignored.
Changing these assumptions would change the conclusions
regarding which strategies dominate. One may also want to
determine preferred strategies for producers with particular
types of objectives--e.g., producers who want to minimize
the risk of falling below a target level of revenue. Under
Fackler's assumptions, one cannot conclude that options
dominate or are dominated by a simple price guarantee
program. Both give the same results if the price is greater
than the guaranteed price. When price is less than the
guaranteed price and quantity is less than the protected
quantity, options give higher revenues. When price is less
than the guaranteed price and quantity is greater than the
protected quantity, a price guarantee program gives higher
revenues. Thus, neither strategy dominates. However, a
producer who wanted to minimize the risk of falling below a
target revenue equal to the quantity protected multiplied by
the strike price would prefer options. The use of options

increases his revenues under the worst conditions even though he gives up some revenue under more favorable conditions.

In the second section of the paper, the cost section, Fackler discusses two problems with market-traded options replacing commodity programs. First, Fackler argues that option sellers may demand sizable risk premiums, making options very expensive relative to the protection provided. The elimination of the price floor would increase the risk of writing puts and thus cause put option premiums to increase. The expected profit from writing puts would have to increase to attract capital to that market. Capital would come because there is no significant barrier to entry into the market to write puts. An information or educational barrier may exist in the short run because many people do not understand option writing and would have to invest the time to learn about it. However, an increase in premiums would increase the incentive to learn. An institutional barrier may also exist because there are limited numbers of members at exchanges, and thus fixed numbers of floor traders. However, exchanges have increased the numbers of members or memberships in the past when they felt more traders were needed. One would expect exchanges to continue this practice in the future.

Some people have argued that premiums would be high because options would be written by a few traders, particularly a few large firms, causing a high concentration of traders on one side of the market. As I understand it, the argument is that the risk associated with writing puts would be less for these firms because of their cash positions. This argument does not seem justified, however, because anyone can duplicate the risk and return of a cash position with a futures position. Thus, option premiums will be competitively determined. Perhaps not initially but after some adjustment period, the expected profits from writing puts will be equal to the expected profits from any other endeavor, after adjusting for differences in risk. Farmers and others may think these premiums are too high for the protection they receive. But the premium should be the competitive market's determination of the revenues necessary to convince someone to bear the risk.

The second problem Fackler discusses regarding options replacing commodity programs is that volume in options would have to increase substantially to provide protection similar to that offered by commodity programs. Volume in options would have to grow substantially. However, the need for volume growth should not be viewed as a problem. Hedging has been recognized as the driving force behind the success of a futures contract. In general, if there is a substantial hedging base, a futures contract will succeed. If hedging orders in soybean options increase significantly, volume will grow to absorb these orders. Volume in the corn and wheat contracts grew substantially between 1970-72 and 1973-74 when hedging needs increased. Volume also increased in 1980 in these contracts for the same reason. One may question which types of traders would write the additional options. Certainly floor traders would write additional put options if the demand to buy puts were to increase significantly. If floor traders are not willing to bear the risk, they can easily reduce their risk by taking additional option positions and/or futures positions. Some traders may trade options instead of futures contracts. The downside risks of writing a put and buying a futures contract are similar. If premiums were to increase, one would expect some traders to prefer writing options to taking futures positions. Therefore, if hedging orders come to the option pits, other volume necessary to provide market liquidity will come also.

The most significant problem with market-traded options replacing commodity programs is ignored by Fackler. Without government intervention, market-traded options cannot be used to support farm prices and thus farm income, as price support programs can. A price support program may guarantee a price above the equilibrium price. However, such a price cannot be guaranteed with a market-traded option.

Fackler next discusses the possibility of the government writing options for producers. This procedure could decrease government expenditures, because farmers would pay for the options. In addition, it could solve the three possible problems discussed above.

In the third section of the paper, Fackler addresses the effects of alternative policies and institutions on quantity decisions and on expected prices. He argues correctly that government programs cause output to be greater than it would be and that price support programs change the distributions of prices and expected prices. He next states that option markets change the distribution of prices. Although that conclusion seems correct, his argument leading to the conclusion is flawed. Fackler argues that the fact that an option market exists indicates that options provide alternatives that did not exist before. Options may indeed provide alternatives that did not exist previously, but an option market could succeed even if options did not provide such alternatives. An option market could exist because that market could be used more cheaply than other markets. The stock index futures market is an example of a market that provides no additional alternatives. The risks and returns of stock index futures contracts could have been duplicated with combinations of stock option contracts that already existed. Stock index futures contracts have been successful at least in part because of the lower transaction costs. Telser (1981) has argued that futures markets exist because they provide essentially the same benefits as forward contracts, at a lower cost. This same basic argument applies to option markets.

In conclusion, Fackler has the basis for an excellent paper. These comments have highlighted those points on which he and I disagree. In general, he has approached a complex problem systematically and correctly. His research has expanded our understanding of the relationship between free market and government mechanisms of transferring risk.

REFERENCES

Telser, Lester G. "Why There Are Organized Futures Markets." Journal of Law and Economics 24(1981):1-22.

4

Stability and Farm Programs:
A Case Study of Feed Grain Markets

Marshall A. Martin

ABSTRACT

For over one-half century the primary goal of U.S. agricultural policy has been to enhance and stabilize farm prices and income. Much of this policy has been directed towards the grains sector. The findings from two research studies offer insights into the stabilization of alternative feed grain policies.

Edelman and Martin used a stochastic model of the U.S. corn and soybean markets to analyze alternative corn programs. Policies which raised loan rates and target prices reduced price and income instability but sharply increased treasury outlays and stock levels.

Dixit and Martin estimated an econometric model of the U.S. coarse grains sector with endogenous policy variables, i.e., loan rates, effective support prices, acreage set-aside, and government-influenced stocks. Major production shocks which affect U.S. export demand had three- to five-year effects on both the market and policy variables.

The current debate on feed grain policy alternatives has focused primarily on price and income levels and government budget outlays and ignored stability considerations. While lower support prices can reduce government budget outlays, such policies can result in greater price and income instability in the feed grain sector.

INTRODUCTION

The variability, not just the level, of farm prices and income has long been a major U.S. farm economic problem. Price and income variability has been caused by business cycles which lead to variation in domestic demand, unstable

---

Associate Professor, Department of Agricultural Economics, Purdue University

world markets which destabilize U.S. export demand, and weather and commodity cycles which influence the supply of farm products.

The primary goals of U.S. agricultural policy for over one-half century have been to enhance and stabilize farm prices and income. The legislation adopted to achieve these goals has been directed primarily towards the grains sector of U.S. agriculture. This paper explores briefly the history of U.S. feed grain programs, documents the stability of prices and income in the agricultural sector--especially the feed grains sector--and analyzes the empirical findings reported in two recent research studies conducted by the author. The paper ends with a few concluding comments.

HISTORY OF FEED GRAIN PROGRAMS

While agricultural price and income instability reemerged as a major problem in the 1970s, the problem dates to the very origins of commercial agriculture. Both the price-inelastic nature of agricultural supply and demand and the basically competitive structure of U.S. agriculture create an economic environment in which, without adequate buffer stocks or other policy measures, commodity prices and farm income will be inherently unstable relative to the nonfarm sector.

For an explanation of current feed grain programs, examining history will provide some insight. U.S. farmers throughout the twentieth century have been concerned about both the level and the variability of grain prices and farm income.

In the 1920s, following a brief period of economic prosperity prior to World War I, grain prices, farm income, and crop land values fell sharply. During this period the concept of parity was born and the first major policy debates on government intervention in commodity markets transpired.

After the Federal Farm Board failed to stabilize prices in the late 1920s by purchasing excess supplies, Congress legislated the Agricultural Adjustment Act in 1933. This legislation contained the same basic U.S. commodity policies that form the core of today's feed grain programs. While the policy instruments have been modified gradually, the two primary goals of (1) price stabilization and (2) raising the level of farm commodity prices and income have remained.

In the 1930s acreage allotments and nonrecourse loans were the principal policy instruments designed to stabilize and raise grain prices and farm income. Despite acreage allotments which reduced wheat and feed grain acreage, yields rose, surpluses accumulated, and farm prices fell. Government programs helped to avert a drastic drop in farm income, however.

During and immediately following World War II, price supports were raised to 90 percent of parity. These price incentives and the rapid adoption of hybrid corn and other production technologies coupled with a decline in demand resulted in an accumulation of stocks owned by the Commodity Credit Corporation (CCC) at the end of the 1940s.

During the 1950s, relatively high price supports, acreage allotments, and a Soil Bank program were used to reduce production. In 1957, 21 million acres were in the acreage reserve and 29 million acres in the conservation reserve. However, given the relative stability of prices and the continued rapid adoption of new output-increasing technology, feed grain production continued to grow. The corn loan rate exceeded the market price every year from 1952 to 1960 and corn stocks accumulated, reaching 2 billion bushels by 1961 (Langley et al., 1985; Tweeten, 1979).

Steps were taken during the 1960s to reduce the accumulation of CCC stocks. Prior to the 1960s, nonrecourse loans were the primary means to guarantee returns to farmers. In 1965, farm legislation separated loan rates from income support payments. Loan rates were reduced to match world market prices more closely, and farm income was supported through direct per-unit payments to farmers, who were required to comply with voluntary acreage reduction programs. While the government outlays for the programs were large, they did reduce production and excess stocks. The programs were popular with farmers and remained the basic form of feed grain programs for the remainder of the 1960s.

In 1962 the Congress debated and almost passed a mandatory farm program. Such a bill narrowly passed in the Senate but was narrowly defeated in the House of Representatives. The final legislative outcome was the continuation of a costly feed grain program and a provision for a wheat referendum in 1963 which, after much heated debate, was defeated by farmers. Until the mid-1980s, when a legislative proposal for a mandatory acreage reduction program was introduced by Senator Harkin (IA) and Congressman Gephardt (MO), little serious consideration had been given to a mandatory farm program since the debate in the early 1960s.

The 1970s issued in a new era in American agriculture with a sharp increase in export sales, an expansion in grain production, and higher farm prices and income during most of the decade. While the Agriculture and Consumer Protection Act of 1973 introduced the concepts of target prices and deficiency payments, they were not implemented--given high commodity prices--until after the passage of the Food and Agricultural Act of 1977. While the increase in agricultural exports in the 1970s did increase farm prices and incomes, it also increased the exposure of U.S. agriculture to the greater uncertainty of international markets. As a means of dealing with the widening swings in prices and incomes, the 1977 Act authorized the Farmer-Owned Reserve program.

A strong U.S. dollar, expanded production in other countries, and a world recession resulted in a sharp decline U.S. grain exports, prices, and farm income in the early 1980s. The immediate governmental response, partially to offset the effects of the 1980 U.S.S.R. grain embargo, was a sharp increase in U.S. stocks owned or influenced by government policy. U.S. corn stocks reached 3.5 billion bushels in 1982-83, declined to 1.0 billion bushels in 1983-84 following a drought and the Payment-in-Kind program in 1983, and currently are projected to exceed 5 billion bushels on October 1, 1987.

The loss of export sales and the subsequent stocks accumulation in the early 1980s also are policy related. The loan rates and target prices legislated in the Agriculture and Food Act of 1981 assumed a continuation of high rates of inflation and no decline in exports (Figure 1). These high support prices encouraged production in the U.S. and in other countries, discouraged U.S. exports, and led to billions of bushels of grain going under CCC nonrecourse loans.

Although Congress did authorize a substantial reduction in loan rates in the Food Security Act of 1985, target prices will remain essentially unchanged until the end of the decade. A modest reduction is authorized beginning in 1988 (about 9 percent reduction for corn over a three-year period from $3.03 to $2.75 per bushel by 1990). Despite high participation rates in the voluntary acreage reduction and conservation reserve programs in 1986 and 1987, modern technology and favorable weather have resulted in near-record feed grain production. In fact, U.S. corn production has surpassed 8 billion bushels in four out of the past six years and in only one of those (1983, when production was 4.2 billion bushels with the Payment-in-Kind program and a drought) was corn production sharply less than

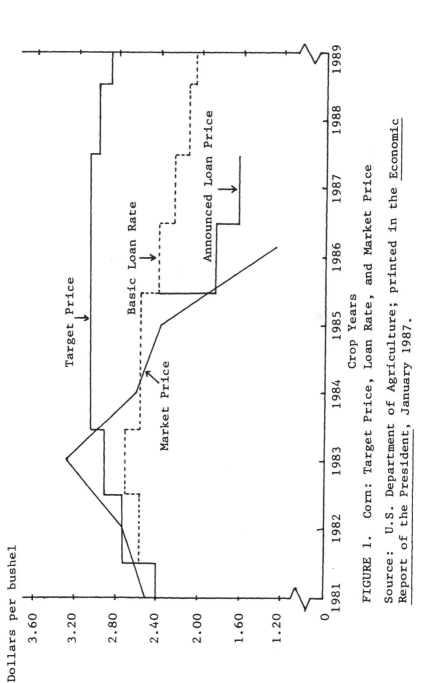

FIGURE 1. Corn: Target Price, Loan Rate, and Market Price

Source: U.S. Department of Agriculture; printed in the Economic
Report of the President, January 1987.

8 billion bushels. This, along with only a modest recent recovery in grain exports, has resulted in large stock levels. Furthermore, government farm program costs have burgeoned, reaching $26 billion last year. Payments to feed grain producers directly through deficiency and paid land diversion payments, nonrecourse loans, and the use of Payment-in-Kind certificates represent a substantial proportion of current government farm progam outlays.

HOW STABLE HAS U.S. AGRICULTURE BEEN?

World and national economic events, government policies, decisions by economic agents, and weather all contribute to the observed performance of the U.S. agricultural sector. Trends and variations in commodity prices and farm income provide a means of evaluating the performance of the agricultural sector. Also trends in and stability of feed grain production, exports, and stocks are of particular interest.

All farm commodity prices in nominal dollars remained relatively constant in the 1960s, rose sharply in the 1970s and have declined since 1984 (Agricultural Outlook, March 1987). In constant 1972 dollars, corn, wheat, and soybean prices fell during most of the 1950s and 1960s, rose sharply in the early 1970s, and have declined steadily over the past 10 years (Figure 2). While crop and livestock prices have followed a similar pattern during the past twenty-five years, livestock prices have not declined as sharply as crop prices in the 1980s.

Nominal commodity prices were much less stable in the 1970s than in the preceeding decade or in the 1980s to date (Table 1). However, feed grain prices were more unstable than crop or livestock prices in the 1970s and 1980s. Livestock prices have been much more stable than feed grain prices in the 1980s.

In real terms the stability of commodity prices exhibits a slightly different pattern than in nominal terms (Table 2). Feed grain prices, while still much more unstable than in the 1960s, were more stable in the 1980s than in the 1970s. The instability of livestock prices increased over the three decades, however. In fact, the increased instability of livestock prices in the 1980s relative to the 1970s more than offset the increased stability of grain prices in the same period, such that the coefficient of variation for the index of all product prices was slightly larger for the 1980s than for the 1970s.

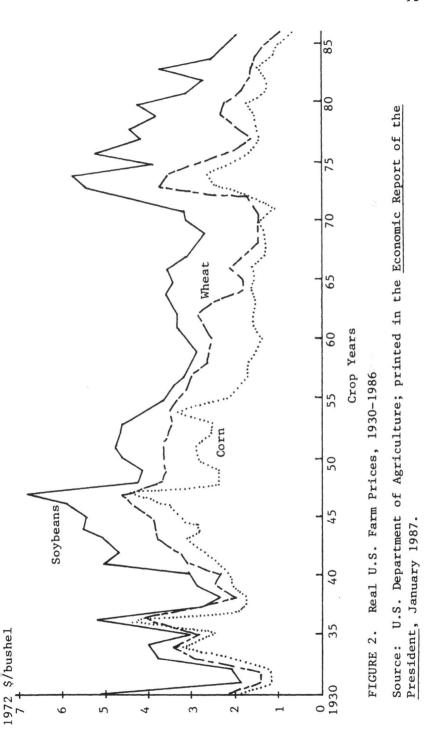

FIGURE 2. Real U.S. Farm Prices, 1930-1986

Source: U.S. Department of Agriculture; printed in the Economic Report of the President, January 1987.

TABLE 1.   Variation in Nominal U.S. Commodity Prices, Farm
Income, Government Payments, and the Feed Grain Sector[a]

Item	Coefficient of Variation in:		
	1960-69	1970-79	1980-86
Index of Prices Received			
All Products	4.5	24.9	4.8
All Crops	3.2	27.6	8.4
Feed Grains	6.1	31.3	14.5
All Livestock	9.7	25.3	2.6
Cash Receipts			
All Crops	8.2	33.9	3.3
Feed Grains	8.2	34.0	12.3
All Livestock	14.5	27.4	2.4
Total without			
Government Payments	11.5	29.7	1.7
Government Payments	41.8	59.1	65.9
Total with Government			
Payments	13.2	28.1	2.4
Feed Grains			
Production	9.8	14.9	20.3
Exports	21.9	35.8	24.1
Ending Stocks	25.6	42.8	54.7

[a]All data used to calculate the coefficients of variation
are from Agricultural Outlook, March 1987.

TABLE 2. Variation in Real U.S. Commodity Prices, Farm
Income, and Government Payments[a]

Item	Coefficient of Variation in:		
	1960-69	1970-79	1980-86
Index of Prices Received			
All Products	5.0	12.4	13.0
All Crops	9.9	18.9	15.3
Feed Grains	8.2	26.2	20.4
All Livestock	4.4	10.7	12.1
Cash Receipts			
All Crops	3.3	20.9	14.3
Feed Grains	11.1	25.6	15.0
All Livestock	6.3	10.3	9.0
Total without Government Payments	3.6	13.6	9.8
Government Payments	35.1	73.6	61.9
Total with Government Payments	5.2	11.9	13.3

[a]All data used to calculate the coefficients of variation
are from Agricultural Outlook, March 1987. All prices and
income data were deflated by the GNP price deflator with a
base of 1982=100 as found in the Economic Report of the
President, January 1987.

Another measure of stability in the agricultural sector is the variation in nominal farm income (Agricultural Outlook, March 1987). Cash receipts for crops and livestock in nominal terms rose steadily during the last twenty-five years, reaching a peak in the early 1980s. Cash receipts for crops (including CCC loans) have averaged about $72 billion in the 1980s and livestock sales have been about $70 billion, resulting in total cash receipts from farming with CCC loans but excluding other government payments of $142 billion. Direct government payments rose from about $1 billion in the early 1960s to $4 billion in the early 1970s. They then fell sharply in the mid-1970s to less than $1 billion and began to rise in the early 1980s, reaching $7.7 billion in 1985. Total cash receipts, including government payments, rose steadily in nominal terms during the past twenty-five years.

In constant dollars, net cash income declined in the early 1950s, remained relatively constant until the early 1970s (when it rose sharply) and has declined since then (Figure 3).

Cash receipts in nominal dollars for crops and livestock were much less stable in the 1970s (Table 1). While the variation in crop and livestock receipts has declined sharply in the 1980s as compared to the 1970s, feed grain receipts have remained more variable than crops or livestock in general. The variation in government payments has increased over the twenty-five-year period. There is little difference in the variation in cash receipts with or without government payments.

Variation in export sales and prices in the 1970s contributed to a large coefficient of variation for both commodity prices and cash receipts. Relatively high loan rates, CCC-funded stocks accumulation, and large government transfer payments helped stabilize nominal farm prices. However, there was growing instability in nominal government outlays. Cash receipts with government payments were less stable than cash receipts without government payments in the 1980s.

Although the general pattern for total cash receipts was the same--with much larger coefficients of variation in the 1970s than in the 1960s in both nominal and real dollars--the variability in nominal dollars was larger than in real dollars in the 1970s (Tables 1 and 2). The opposite was true in the 1980s. In fact, in real dollars, total cash receipts with government payments were slightly less stable in the 1980s than in the 1970s. The opposite was the case for cash receipts without government payments,

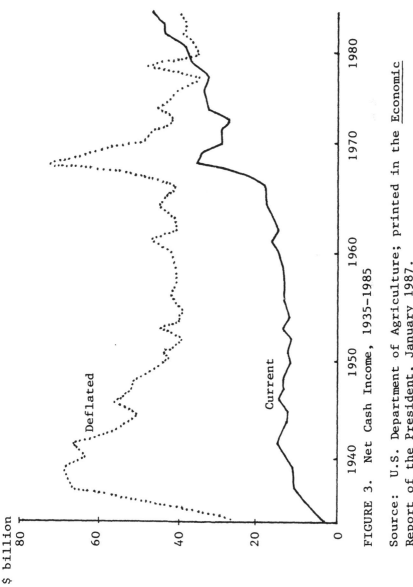

FIGURE 3. Net Cash Income, 1935-1985

Source: U.S. Department of Agriculture; printed in the Economic Report of the President, January 1987.

suggesting that government payments helped stabilize farm income in the 1970s and destabilize it in the 1980s.

Instability in the feed grain sector has tended to increase over the past twenty-five years (Table 1). The coefficients of variation for both feed grain production and ending stocks have increased since the 1960s. The coefficient of variation for feed grain exports was larger in the 1970s than in the 1960s or 1980s, however.

SOME EMPIRICAL FINDINGS

While analysis of the coefficients of variation for selected variables for different time periods can be enlightening, it is difficult to isolate the influences of different economic events or policies on the stability of commodity prices and farm income. Estimation of econometric models and simulation of different policies using counterfactual analysis can provide insights into economic behavior. The empirical results from two such studies of the U.S. feed grain sector are reported below.

In 1983 Edelman and Martin published a study which analyzed the effects of selected farm commodity programs on U.S. corn and soybean markets. Using a multi-year, stochastic partial equilibrium model developed by Holland and Meekhof (1979), they analyzed the following policy options: continuation of the 1979 feed grain program, elimination of deficiency payments, elimination of all commodity programs, a high loan rate, a high loan rate and target price, and a moderate set-aside with a moderate target price (Table 3). The model contained stochastic yield and export demand equations. Acreage was influenced by relative prices and the set-aside program. Public and private stocks were influenced by market prices and farm program parameters. Domestic use was a function of market prices for feed and behavior of the livestock sector.

The 1979 program did not require farmers to set aside any acreage to receive program benefits. In 1979 dollars the loan rate was $2.10 and the target price $2.20 per bushel. The no-deficiency-payment option had the same policy parameters as the 1979 program except that the target price and deficiency payments were eliminated. The free market case removed all price and income supports and sold all CCC stocks. The high-loan-rate scenario held the target price at $2.20 but increased the loan rate to $2.42 per bushel. Thus, the target price/deficiency payment program became inoperative. Under the high target price and loan rate option the target price was set at $2.75 and the loan

TABLE 3. Parameters for Alternative Policy Scenarios, 1979 Real Prices

	Policy Parameters[a]					
Simulation	Target Price	Loan Rate	FOR Release[b]	FOR Call[b]	CCC Release	Program Partici- pation
	------ $/bu. -------					%
1979 Program	2.20	2.10	2.63	3.05	3.15	90
No Deficiency Payments	0	2.10	2.63	3.05	3.15	90
Free Market	0	0	0	0	0	0
High Loan Rate	2.20	2.42	3.02	3.45	3.80	90
High Target Price and Loan Rate	2.75	2.42	3.02	3.45	3.80	90
Set-Aside and Moderate Target Price	2.53	2.10	2.63	3.05	3.15	50

Source: Edelman and Martin (1983).

[a]The national allocation factor is assumed to be 0.9. The annual farmer-owned reserve (FOR) storage payment is $0.265 per bushel and the maximum amount in the farmer-owned reserve is 1,000 million bushels. The Commodity Credit Corporation (CCC) interest rate is assumed to be 12 percent.

[b]The 1981 Act replaces the FOR release and call price concept with a single trigger price mechanism. Since the relative relationship between the reserve trigger mechanism and the loan rate is similar to that in the old legislation, the simulation results may vary slightly but the conclusions would not be altered.

rate at $2.42 per bushel in 1979 dollars. The set-aside option reduced harvested corn acreage by about 2 million acres and set the target price at $2.53 per bushel in 1979 dollars.

For purposes of this paper, only the results for the zero rate of growth in export demand are reported (Table 4). For each policy scenario the model was simulated for the period 1979 through 1986 with 300 iterations per year.

If the 1979 program had been followed, with no export growth during the past seven years, the effective mean price for corn (including any deficiency payment) would have been $2.70 per bushel with a coefficient of variation of 19 percent. The soybean price would have been $7.09 per bushel with a coefficient of variation of 24 percent. The probability that government payments would have exceeded $1 billion would have been less than 1 percent. Price levels and variation would have been similar if the deficiency payments were eliminated but direct government outlays would have declined to zero.

A free market, even with the assumed zero growth in foreign demand, would have resulted in slightly higher expected prices, once the stocks were released, but also greater price variation (a coefficient of variation of 30 percent for the price of corn and 26 percent for soybeans). There would have been no government payments, of course.

A high loan rate would have increased the corn price by about 3 percent but reduced the coefficient of variation to 15 percent. There would have been no government deficiency payments, but government outlays for stocks would have increased as stock levels rose to over 2 billion bushels.

As expected, increasing support prices would have resulted in higher cash receipts, including government payments and higher government payments as compared to the free market, or elimination of deficiency payment options. A high target price and loan rate would have increased the corn price by 8 percent in comparison to the continuation of the 1979 program. It also would have reduced the coefficient of variation to 14 percent but increased to 54 percent the probability that the annual deficiency payments for corn would exceed $1 billion. With a set-aside which reduced corn acres by 2 million acres (about 3 percent) and more moderate target price and loan rate levels, corn prices would have been about 5 percent above the 1979 program case and the price variation about the same. The probability that annual corn deficiency payments would exceed $1 billion would have been 23 percent. Corn stock levels would still have exceeded 2 billion bushels, however.

The Edelman and Martin study clearly indicates that increased government intervention in the feed grain sector can increase commodity price levels and reduce price variation. However, this requires substantial increases in government treasury costs and CCC stocks. Furthermore, changes in feed grain programs influence soybean production, stocks, and price level and variation.

They conclude their study as follows:

> The need for government intervention via commodity programs in the decade of the 1980s will be very sensitive to changes in foreign and domestic supply and demand relationships. Variations in export demand growth can result in substantial fluctuations in commodity prices, farm income, and stock levels. Policies must be designed that provide program flexibility that can respond to changing market conditions without causing excessive uncertainty for farmers, agribusiness firms, and others affected by farm commodity programs.
>
> The empirical results contained in this study suggest that while high price supports can enhance farm income and reduce price variation, they usually require large Treasury outlays. While no commodity programs or low price support levels can reduce Treasury outlays, they usually result in substantial variation in farm prices and income unless export demand continues to grow at fairly rapid rates. (pp. 11-12)

The actual observed real price of corn in 1979 dollars for the period 1979-1986 was $2.09 per bushel with a coefficient of variation of 19 percent. For soybeans the real price was $5.10 per bushel with a coefficient of variation of 23 percent. The real observed prices of corn and soybeans in the period 1979-1986 were lower than those for any of the scenarios analyzed by Edelman and Martin. Sharp declines in U.S. export demand, record U.S. and world production, and a substantial reduction in loan rates in the Food Security Act of 1985 all contributed to lower market prices. However, while the coefficient of variation for soybeans was similar to those in all the scenarios analyzed by Edelman and Martin, the actual coefficient of variation was less than for the free market scenario but larger than for the high loan rate and target price scenarios.

TABLE 4. Simulated Average Annual Government Costs, Price Levels and Variation, and Production and Value under Zero Export Demand Growth, 1979/80 - 1985/86[a]

Simulation Characteristics	Units
Average Annual Treasury Costs:	
1. Deficiency Payments	$mil
2. Total Producer Payments[b]	$mil
3. Total Treasury Outlays[c]	$mil
4. Frequency of $3 billion in Total Treasury Outlays	percent
Average Annual Prices:	
5. Corn: Effective Price Level[d]	$/bu
6. Deficiency Payment Rate	$/bu
7. Standard Deviation	$/bu
8. Coefficient of Variation	percent
9. Frequency of Market Price Below $2.50/bu	percent
10. Soybeans: Price Level	$/bu
11. Standard Deviation	$/bu
12. Coefficient of Variation	percent
13. Frequency of Market Price Below $6.50/bu	percent
Average Production and Value:	
14. Corn: Production	mil bu
15. Total Carryout Stocks[e]	mil bu
16. Value of Production Plus Deficiency Payments	$bil
17. Deficiency Payments as a Percent of Total Value[f]	percent
18. Frequency of Exceeding $1 billion in Deficiency Payments	percent
19. Soybeans: Production	mil bu
20. Total Carryout Stocks	mil bu
21. Value of Production	$bil
22. Total Value of Corn and Soybean Production[f]	$bil
23. Deficiency Payments as a Percent of Total Value[f]	percent

(Table 4, continued)

1979 Program	No Deficiency Payments	Free Market	High Loan Rate	High Target Price and Loan Rate	Set-Aside and Moder- ate Target Price[g]
115.1	0.0	0.0	0.0	1255.4	442.7
242.6	126.2	10.2	192.7	1457.4	558.4
539.0	411.8	12.3	1233.1	2759.2	738.9
4.0	1.6	0.0	11.0	40.4	7.1
2.70	2.68	2.71	2.78	2.91	2.83
.02	.00	.00	.00	.17	.12
.52	.52	.81	.42	.40	.53
19	20	30	15	14	19
39.7	40.8	44.0	40.6	46.2	38.7
7.09	7.08	7.11	7.19	7.29	7.15
1.67	1.67	1.86	1.64	1.65	1:68
24	24	26	23	23	24
42.3	42.8	44.0	38.8	36.5	40.9
7871	7862	7832	7934	8049	7809
1391	1377	787	2182	2467	1260
21.21	21.07	21.22	22.06	23.31	21.61
0.5	0.0	0.0	0.0	5.4	2.0
0.1	0.0	0.0	0.0	54.2	23.2
2197	2199	2199	2191	2170	2191
307	307	307	305	304	306
15.58	15.57	15.64	15.76	15.82	15.67
36.79	36.64	36.86	37.82	39.13	37.28
0.3	0.0	0.0	0.0	3.2	1.2

(Table 4, continued)

Source: Adapted from data in Edelman and Martin (1983).

[a]Based on 300 iterations over a seven-year period, 1979/80 through 1985/86.   Assumes annual yield growth rates: corn 2 bu, soybeans 0.5 bu; annual domestic demand growth rates: corn 2%, soybeans 5%; annual export demand growth rates: corn and soybeans, 0%.

[b]Deficiency payments plus farmer-owned reserve storage payments.

[c]Total producer payments plus net Commodity Credit Corporation costs.

[d]Market price plus deficiency payment rate.

[e]Private stocks plus Farmer-Owned Reserve and Commodity Credit Corporation Stocks.

[f]Total value includes market value plus deficiency payments for corn.

[g]Average acreage set-aside equals 3.3 million acres or 4.0 percent of total corn acreage.

A second study by Dixit and Martin (1986) simulated the influence on the behavior of the U.S. course grains sector of weather and other factors beyond farmers' or policy-makers' control. Dixit and Martin used an econometric model of the U.S. coarse grains sector which contained supply and demand equations for corn and other coarse grains. A unique feature of the model was the inclusion of the endogenous determination of the value of the policy variables. The model contained thirty-three equations divided into supply, demand, trade, and policy blocks (Figure 4). They simulated the effects of weather shocks within the U.S., and in other countries, on the U.S. coarse grains sector. They also compared the legislated loan rates in the 1981 Agriculture and Food Act to a three-year moving average method. Their basic conclusions can be summarized as follows:

> Major changes in domestic production can dramatically alter the environment in which policy decisions are made. A major production shortfall or a bumper crop can affect government policy decisions for nearly 5 years, even though the entire domestic supply and demand structure returns to equilibrium within 3 years.
> Extreme changes in the export economy are required to bring about changes in government programs. Although limiting total stocks in the Farmer-Owned Reserve may solve problems associated with large accumulation of government-owned grain stocks, a ceiling on the reserve could mean lower market prices and larger price support payments.
> A moving average method for setting loan rates should provide definitive, timely information for establishing those rates, lower domestic and world prices, and provide greater shortrun stability. (p. v)

Two findings in the Dixit and Martin study are especially noteworthy for this conference on stability. First, exogenous shocks such as weather factors in the U.S. or unexpected changes in U.S. export demand not only influence market prices for several years but also cause legislative and administrative changes in policy variables for as long as five years. These conclusions are based on the behavior of the endogenous policy variables such as loan rates and effective price supports for the period 1960

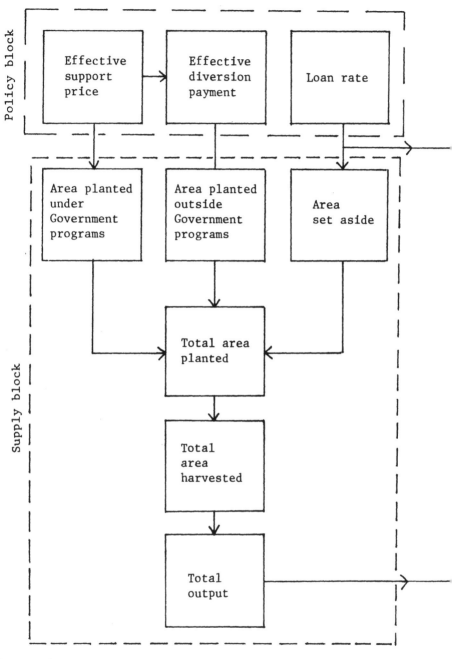

FIGURE 4.   A One-Period Schematic of the Aggregated U.S.
            Course Grains Market

Source: Dixit and Martin (1986).

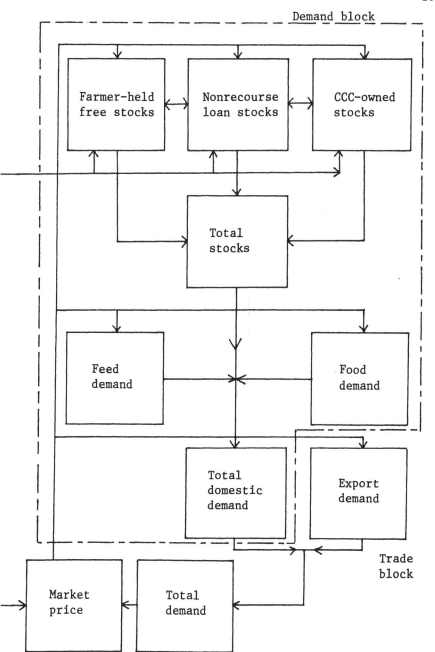

through 1981.   Second, a moving average method for
establishing loan rates could increase price stability for
the coarse grains sector.

SOME CONCLUDING COMMENTS

Historically, the primary source of instability
in the U.S. agricultural sector has been unexpected weather
events in the U.S.   However, in recent years macroeconomic
policies and government policy decisions in the U.S.
and in other countries have added a new dimension of
uncertainty to grain markets.

Although the variability in prices and incomes was
somewhat less in the early 1980s than in the 1970s, there
was much less stability in the feed grain sector than was
experienced in the 1960s.   Also the declines in commodity
prices, farm income, exports, and land values have placed
strong financial pressure on many farmers, making them very
vulnerable to any unexpected changes in commodity markets or
to government decisions that might further adversely affect
them.

The Edelman and Martin study suggests that there are
some clear trade-offs between the level of government price
supports and farm price and income stability, especially
when there is little growth in export demand.   Furthermore,
as indicated by the Dixit and Martin findings, government
policy decisions may continue to reflect previous economic
events for a period of several years.   This may add
additional uncertainty to markets.   A moving average method
for determining loan rates is one means of removing
arbitrary government policy actions and adding some
short-run price stability.   Also if loan rates more
effectively reflect market equilibrium prices, there
should be more efficient allocation of resources and the
U.S. should be more competitive in world markets.

Much of the current policy debate on a mandatory
acreage set-aside program, decoupling, and minor
modifications in the 1985 Act (such as more rapid reduction
in target price levels) has focused on price and income
levels, export response, and government cost implications.
There has been relatively little discussion on the sectoral
stability implications of these policy alternatives.   Given
the history of instability of commodity prices and farm
income and the increased sources of instability in an
increasingly interdependent global economy, the stability
implications of alternative feed grain programs merit the
attention of policy analysts and policy-makers.

REFERENCES

Agricultural Outlook. Yearbook Issue. Washington,
    D.C.: U.S. Department of Agriculture, Economic Research
    Service, March 1987.
Council of Economic Advisers. Economic Report of the
    President. Washington, D.C.: GPO, January 1987.
Dixit, Praveen M. and Marshall A. Martin. Policymaking for
    U.S. Commodity Programs: A Case Study of the Coarse
    Grains Sector. Washington, D.C.: U.S. Department of
    Agriculture, Economic Research Service, Foreign
    Agricultural Economic Report No. 219, 1986.
Edelman, Mark A. and Marshall A. Martin. An Analysis of
    U.S. Farm Commodity Program Alternatives for Corn and
    Soybean Programs Under Different Export Growth
    Scenarios. Purdue University Agricultural Experiment
    Station Bulletin No. 408, 1983.
Holland, Forrest D. and Ronald L. Meekhof. FEEDSIM
    Description and Computer Program Documentation. Purdue
    University Agricultural Experiment Station Bulletin
    No. 221, 1979.
Langley, James A. et al. "Commodity and Income Support
    Perspectives." In Agricultural-Food Policy Review:
    Commodity Program Perspectives. Washington, D.C.: USDA,
    Economic Research Service, Agricultural Economic Report
    No. 530, 1985, pp. 122-165.
Tweeten, Luther. Foundations of Farm Policy, 2nd ed. rev.
    Lincoln: University of Nebraska Press, 1979.

Reaction

Randall A. Kramer

Martin has presented a useful discussion of instability and farm programs as experienced in the feed grains sector. I will discuss a few aspects of his paper and add a few comments.

Martin begins with a summary of feed grain legislation since the 1950s. We are reminded that some of the farm problems of the 1950s (such as surpluses and low income) and policy instruments of the 1950s (such as acreage allotments and conservation reserves) are once again a part of the current farm policy dialogue.

Martin next addresses the question: How stable has U.S. agriculture been? He answers this by considering estimated coefficients of variation. I would offer one note of caution about the use of the coefficient of variation. Although it is an appropriate way to measure instability, as Martin has done, it is not a good measure of risk, despite its use for that purpose in some of the literature. There is an important distinction between risk and instability which is frequently overlooked. If one wishes to measure risk, one must measure variations around producers' expectations, rather than around an historical mean.

Martin presents coefficients of variation for a number of different data series, and provides further evidence that agricultural markets exhibited considerably more instability in the 1970s than during the 1960s or 1980s. In an examination of his Table 1, one comparison of particular interest emerges. Comparing the coefficient of variation

Associate Professor, Department of Agricultural Economics, Virginia Polytechnic Institute and State University.

for cash receipts from feed grains to that from livestock, in each case the variability is greater for feed grains. The United States has a long history of regulating feed grain markets, but not livestock markets. Yet in spite of these interventions, cash receipts from feed grains have continued to be more variable than cash receipts from livestock. Perhaps this is because of inherent differences between the two types of markets; in particular, a larger proportion of grain than livestock production is traded internationally.

When one examines these figures on variation in the context of the title of this conference, it is logical to ask: Would variation have been greater or smaller in the absence of farm programs? Although Martin does not address this question directly, some recent work I have done with McDowell and Price (1986) sheds some light on this issue. We used the Economic Research Service's policy analysis model, FAPSIM, to examine some alternative approaches to farm programs. In the process of doing that work, we generated some estimates of the effects of past programs on farm income variability. Admittedly, using an econometric model to simulate time series on net farm income in the absence of farm programs requires some strong assumptions, but there is no alternative since a counterfactual historical data series does not exist. In our analysis, it was found that for the period 1970-1982, the simulated "free market" net farm income for the United States had a coefficient of variation of 30 percent. This compares with a coefficient of variation of 25 percent for the actual historical period. Thus, there is evidence that farm programs made net farm income more stable during the 1970s than it otherwise might have been. Does this provide economic justification for the programs? Not necessarily, because the benefits of increased stabilization may be offset by the cost of the programs. For example, in an analysis of the Farmer-Owned Reserve Program, Just (1981) concluded that the benefits of short-run stabilization were not sufficient to outweigh the costs of the program.

Turning back to Martin's paper: in the last section he discusses two empirical studies in which he has been involved. The first one looks at the effects through the mid-1980s of changes in target prices and loan rates for corn (Edelman and Martin, 1979). The results are discussed in relation to the status quo. I believe that it would be more enlightening to compare the effects of these policy changes to those of the programs which were actually in effect. I realize that it was not possible to make this comparison at the time the study was completed, but now that the time of reference of the analysis has passed, one could go back and do so.

Finally, Martin discusses another, more recent study which analyzed the political determination of loan rates and target prices. I was particularly interested in Dixit and Martin's (1986) finding that a 33-percent shortfall in production could affect policy decisions for as long as five years. This helps explain why we see so much instability in farm programs. The profession has just scratched the surface on endogenized policy variables in econometric models. Dixit and Martin have made an important contribution to this work. I believe that much can be learned from more research on this important topic.

REFERENCES

Dixit, Praveen M., and Marshall A. Martin. _Policymaking for U.S. Commodity Programs: A Case Study of the Coarse Grains Sector_. Washington, D.C.: U.S. Department of Agriculture, Economic Research Service, Foreign Agricultural Economic Report No. 219, 1986.

Edelman, Mark A., and Marshall A. Martin. _An Analysis of U.S. Farm Commodity Program Alternatives for Corn and Soybean Programs Under Different Export Growth Scenarios_. Purdue University Agricultural Experiment Station Bulletin No. 408, 1983.

Just, Richard E. _Farmer-Owned Grain Reserve Program Needs Modification to Improve Effectiveness: Theoretical and Empirical Considerations in Agricultural Buffer Stock Policy Under the Food and Agriculture Act of 1977_. Washington, D.C.: U.S. General Accounting Office, CED-81-70, June 26, 1981.

McDowell, Howard, Randall A. Kramer, and Michael Price. "A Sector Income Support and Risk Bearing Policy for Agriculture." Paper presented at the American Association for Advancement of Science meetings, Philadelphia, PA, May 28, 1986.

5

Stability and the Tobacco Program

Daniel A. Sumner

ABSTRACT

This analysis of stability in the U.S. tobacco industry examines the causes and consequences of variability of tobacco prices, quantities, input demands, total revenues, costs, and net revenues. I focus on the role of the U.S. tobacco program and the effects of regulatory change. The first step is to describe briefly the industry and the program. Some information about recent patterns of prices and other variables is then presented.

The tobacco program kept variability of the real price of tobacco at a minimum for decades. From 1950 through 1983 the coefficient of variation (c.v.) of the price of tobacco was only about 4 percent, as compared to a c.v. of around 20 percent for other major field crops. But this history does not tell the full story. The output price stability was accompanied by considerable variability in effective quota levels, total revenue, quota lease rates, and returns to quota.

Estimates of supply and demand elasticities, storage costs, and inherent variability of demand suggest that with no program, price and revenue variability in U.S. tobacco would have remained considerably lower than that in other commodities.

The last five years have been a unique period of regulatory instability in tobacco. Program risk as exhibited in sales prices for

Senior Economist, Council of Economic Advisers, Executive Office of the President; and Professor, Department of Economics and Business, North Carolina State University. At the time this paper was prepared, the author was on leave as a Resident Fellow, National Center for Food and Agricultural Policy, Resources for the Future. This paper has grown out of some research on tobacco regulation cited below that was done jointly with Julian M. Alston.

quota has been high. Changes instituted in 1986 seem to have returned stability to the program. However, the risk of a major price decline or other major program change seems to have remained.

This paper does not provide a definitive analysis of the impact of the U.S. tobacco program on stability in the tobacco industry. The detailed research upon which to build such analysis has not been done.

INTRODUCTION

Economists have long discussed farm programs in the context of their impact on stabilization (Johnson, 1976; Schultz, 1953). Most research studies year-to-year movements in output price. The variability and unpredictability of weather and the inelasticity of supply and demand curves generally are seen to be the sources of inherent agricultural instability. Earlier chapters in this volume have considered various aspects of the stability question and a variety of stylized farm programs. The chapter on the feed grains industry has provided an example for a "typical" U. S. program. The tobacco program and the tobacco industry are quite different from the typical case but the program has also been justified as reducing an inherently unstable industry.

This analysis of stability in the U.S. tobacco industry examines the causes and consequences of variability of tobacco prices, quantities, input demands, total revenues, costs, and net revenues. An unregulated tobacco industry is often asserted to be particularly unstable (Marshall, Loyd and Shuffett, 1987). I focus on the role of the U.S. tobacco program and the effects of regulatory change. The first step is to describe briefly the industry and the program. Some information about recent patterns of prices and other variables is then presented.

This paper does not provide a final definitive analysis of the impact of the U.S. tobacco program on stability in the tobacco industry. The extensive background research upon which to build such an analysis is not available.

BACKGROUND: THE TOBACCO INDUSTRY AND THE TOBACCO PROGRAM

The U.S. tobacco industry consists of a number of related leaf tobacco types and several end uses. However, about 92 percent of the U.S. leaf is of the flue-cured and burley types that are the focus of this paper. About 4 percent of the total is represented by minor types grown in the same general region of the Southeast as the two major types. About 3 percent is cigar tobacco, and the rest is type 32 air-cured tobacco, which is grown mostly in Maryland.

Domestic and foreign cigarette manufacturing claims almost all of the flue-cured, burley, and Maryland tobacco. The minor types are used mostly in making cigars or "smokeless" products. The government programs for flue-cured and burley are based on mandatory poundage quotas and price supports. Mandatory acreage allotments are used in the other types, except for the Maryland and Pennsylvania seed types, which are not regulated.

The United States is the world's largest exporter and importer of tobacco. U.S. cigarettes are made from a blend of tobacco types, including oriental, which is not grown in this country. Over the last two decades, however, the United States also has been importing growing quantities of nonoriental types that substitute for U.S.-grown leaf. The significance of foreign competition in both domestic and foreign markets is one of the key features of the leaf tobacco industry (see Sumner and Alston, 1987). Imports and exports coexist because there are significant differences in tobacco characteristics and price.

The major components of the U.S. tobacco program have been in place for fifty years. These major components include:

(1) A loan rate that provides a price floor for each type and grade. The loan rate is supported by government-sponsored stock acquisitions for any tobacco not taken by private buyers. These stocks are later released in direct sales.

(2) Mandatory supply controls that assign to individual farms an amount of acres planted or output that may be sold during the year. Adjustments in these supply controls generally have kept government stocks within bounds.

(3) Some provisions for transferring production rights to other farms with the restriction that tobacco is produced in the county to which the output originally was assigned.

There have been a number of significant changes in the programs in the last five decades, but the essentials have remained in place. In fact, the tobacco program has been as stable as any agricultural commodity program in the world. Later I will discuss changes in program rules and parameters, but first I will illustrate the operation of the basic program (for more detail and analysis see Sumner and Alston, 1986).

Figure 1 provides the basic supply and demand picture for an industry with a quota/price support program. The upward-sloping line labeled MC is the underlying market supply function that shows marginal cost of production at each output level. The downward-sloping demand function, D, includes domestic use, exports and the current demand for stock accumulation. The vertical line illustrates the aggregate mandatory quota set by the government. The horizontal line labeled SP represents the support price also set by the regulations.

The quota and price support levels usually have been set early in the crop year before planting. The rules for adjusting price supports and quotas were changed in 1986 but remain tied to estimates of the demand and supply conditions made by USDA regulators. Prior to 1982, rules for setting price support and quota had been very stable and allowed accurate prediction well in advance of harvest or even planting. These rules generally kept year-to-year price and output adjustment relatively small. From 1982 to 1986, there were changes each year and deviations from the accepted price support formula. The 1986 law seems to have begun another era of relative stability in the program itself.

The actual market price and quantity depend on weather and market conditions that are observed after the setting of price supports and quotas. In seasons when demand is above that expected by regulators, the market price exceeds the support price by more than a historical average. This is also true for seasons in which yields are low so that marketings fall below quota levels.

The market average price for tobacco also depends on the average quality of the crop. There are larger quality-based price differences for tobacco than for any other major field crop. A wide range of prices is received for different lots of tobacco of the same type in every year based on the stalk position and other characteristics of the tobacco leaf. The proportion of tobacco represented by each grade is different from year to year, and this quality variation affects the market average price relative to the preseason average support price.

With the price supports and quotas in place, the market price and quantity variability depends on the variability of the program parameters and on the supply and demand variation that occurs after the policy announcements. The position of the market without the quota and price support program is indicated in Figure 1 by quantity Q_u and price P_u. Variation in these depends directly on the variation and elasticity of the underlying supply and demand functions.

THE SOURCES AND EXTENT OF VARIABILITY EXPECTED FOR TOBACCO

This section discusses how shifts in the supply and demand functions illustrated in Figure 1 affect variability in the tobacco industry. The appendix uses a simple algebraic model to show, more explicitly, how variance of the underlying functions relates to variance of prices, quantities, revenues and costs.

Without a program, demand shocks--movements in the downward-sloping curve, D, in Figure 1--show up in market price and quantity variation and imply total revenue and factor market variation. Because of factor price shifts or yield variation, shocks to the supply function (movements in the upward-sloping curve, MC, in Figure 1) also directly affect market price and quantities. They have both direct and indirect (through output price) effects on revenue and factor markets.

With a quota program, anticipated demand changes influence the support price, and unanticipated demand shifts are reflected in the market price-support price differential. The anticipated demand shifts also influence the basic quota quantity and affect revenues and factor markets through these intermediaries. Anticipated demand changes affect the lease rate for quota through their effect on the expected price and the quota. Shocks to the marginal cost function do not directly affect price or quota quantity. However, anticipated shifts up in factor prices that increase measured average costs increase the support price (with a lag) through the legislated formula. Yield shocks affect the amount by which market price exceeds the support price and affects over-or-under quota sales. Lease rates are affected directly by anticipated shifts in the marginal cost function.

Under the quota program, effects of changes in underlying economic factors are filtered through the mechanisms by which the federal policy is implemented. Shifts in supply or demand may cause movements along the policy response functions. The program can also add potential variation because there may be changes, legislative or administrative, in the program operation or changes in the policy rules themselves. In tobacco, major changes since 1981 include: (a) the legalization of sale of

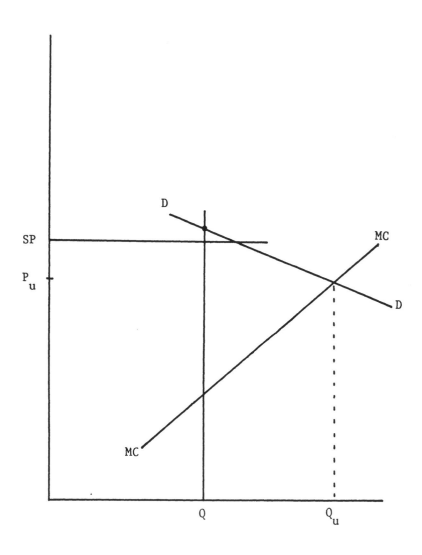

FIGURE 1.   An Illustration of the Tobacco Market
with a Support Price and Quota

quota, (b) the institution of and changes in grower and
buyer assessments, (c) changes in allowance for
overproduction, (d) changes in the rules for setting quotas,
(e) changes in the formulas for adjusting price supports,
and (f) the elimination of leasing of flue-cured quotas.
These changes have been in addition to changes in the levels
of price support and quotas.

Variability of the Underlying Functions

There are two sources of year-to-year variability in
the supply of most agricultural products. The first is
yield variability, causing deviations of actual output from
planned output. In an unregulated tobacco market this would
be augmented by effects of changes in input use due to
changes in planned output, reflected mainly in changes in
acreage. In the current regulated tobacco industry, changes
in planned output are limited by policy, but policy-directed
year-to-year changes in total quota remain as a source of
variability in planned output. Acreage variation has been
substantial for most major agricultural commodities, but
producers and other market participants have at least one
growing season to prepare for variation from this source.
Yield variability is the major source of unanticipated
supply variability at present and would most likely remain
the major source of year-to-year variability in an
unregulated tobacco market. Deregulation would allow more
geographic concentration of the industry, which could
cause greater yield variability as a higher proportion of
the total crop would be subject to more similar growing
conditions. However, the coastal plain, where flue-cured
production would concentrate, has a lower coefficient of
variation of yields than the old and middle belts that would
lose flue-cured acreage under deregulation.
The demand for U.S. tobacco is derived from the demand
for cigarettes in the United States and elsewhere. Overall
cigarette demand does not fluctuate much around long-term
trends. U.S. tobacco demand variability depends also on
variability of foreign tobacco supply, which affects both
import supply and export demand. Import supply and export
demand also vary with changes in the currency exchange rate
and with changes in foreign policies. Although one would
expect larger variability in the foreign trade components of
demand than in the domestic component, U.S. tobacco trade
has in fact fluctuated relatively little around its
long-term trends. Tobacco is grown throughout the world,
but major importers often grow little tobacco. The number

of major exporters has expanded in recent years so that no country has a large share in the trade. There are no recent instances of serious demand variability for tobacco due to political interventions in trade, but there are for other goods. For example, the political turmoil surrounding Zimbabwe was favorable for U.S. tobacco producers but was not a major factor, whereas the embargo on grain imports to the USSR in 1979 had dramatic short-term effects on U.S. grain producers.

The Magnitude of Supply and Demand Elasticities

The tobacco industry is relatively small and uses land intensively so that one would expect highly elastic factor supply to tobacco compared to many industries. This implies that marginal costs rise only slightly when output expands. See Sumner and Alston (1986) and Goodwin, Sumner and Sparrow (1987) for further discussion and empirical results supporting an intermediate-run elasticity of supply of 5.0 or more.

In recent years, around 40 percent of U.S. tobacco production has been exported, while 30 percent of U.S. tobacco consumption has been imported. International trade in tobacco and tobacco products increases the demand elasticity for U.S. tobacco. Econometric work (Sumner and Alston, 1987) suggests a demand elasticity of -2 for current demand. This is much greater than the demand elasticities for most U.S. farm products that depend more on domestic markets. Any responsiveness of storage demand to current price would add to the overall elasticity of demand facing the tobacco industry.

The responsiveness of storage to year-to-year price variability depends on costs of storage and the flexibility of storage. (Interest costs relative to market prices are the same across commodities, so I will focus on other factors.) For the major grain crops, physical storage costs relative to price are much higher than for tobacco. Recent storage charges for wheat, for example, are in the range of about $0.60 per hundredweight per year, plus in-and-out charges. For tobacco, the comparable figure is about $0.66 per hundredweight per year (dry weight) (USDA/ ASCS, personal communication, 1986). However, wheat storage costs are about 10 percent of recent market prices of $6.00 per hundredweight. For tobacco the comparable price is $250 per hundredweight, and direct storage costs are a trivial 0.25 percent of market price.

For grains, expected price changes of at least 10 percent above interest rates of 5 to 10 percent would be required for profitable speculative storage responses. For tobacco, expected percentage price movements would only need to exceed interest rates slightly for storage to respond. The result is that storage is a more effective insulator of price movements for tobacco than for most other commodities.

In summary: supply and demand for tobacco are likely to be less variable year-to-year than for many other traded or nontraded agricultural goods. And, as discussed above, due to the relatively small size of the tobacco industry and the intensity of factor use in production, over any length of run one would expect tobacco supply to be elastic compared to most products; due to the importance of international trade one would expect demand for U.S. tobacco to be relatively elastic, too. Further, relative to value, tobacco is inexpensive to store compared to most other agricultural products, and one would expect year-to-year storage to smooth total demand. Thus any variability in the supply and demand schedules would be reflected more in quantity adjustments (and more on inventory than on consumption) than in prices for tobacco compared to other farm products.

Reactions to Increased Price Variability

Farmers do not simply accept changes in the economic environment; they adjust their behavior in response. How might a tobacco grower react to an increase in the variability of tobacco prices? First, the grower would attempt to predict the path of prices more accurately and adjust by planting more in the high-price years and less in the low-price years. It is even possible to make some adjustments within a season after prices become known. For example, the grower may reduce irrigation or harvest labor when it becomes known that the tobacco price will be low for that season. If adjustments are particularly successful, he may gain income from variable prices as compared to constant prices. Only those cases of increased variability for which accurate prediction is not possible raise potential problems. Only when production is held stable do variable prices imply that gross and net incomes are more variable.

With no change in long-term expected production, the farmer may adjust to the increased variability by increasing his level of borrowing in bad years and lending (or saving and investing) in good years. In the simplest case the sole cost of income variability derives from the additional cost of borrowing over lending. When this differential is low there is little net effect on wealth from the more variable prices. The major bad effect of variability in income results when credit lines are strained and the farm faces liquidation. This occurs not because of simple year-to-year variability but because of longer periods of sustained low returns.

Another reaction to more variable tobacco prices is to reduce the total effect on income variability by reducing the share of tobacco in the portfolio. The farmer will diversify. He may do this by leasing rather than buying quota, by growing more of other crops, and by working or investing capital off the farm.

The variety of available adjustments and their relative cost or payoff determine the losses implied by an increase in variability. If a relatively low-cost way to avoid bad effects of instability is available then it may be of little importance to eliminate the source of the instability. This common-sense approach is often ignored when economists measure only output price variability and fail to model farm behavior in the face of variability.

EVIDENCE OF TOBACCO INDUSTRY VARIABILITY

Table 1, adapted from Sumner and Alston (1986), provides some background on year-to-year variability for yields, acreage, production, and deflated prices for the U.S. tobacco industry and some other major agricultural commodities. Percentage deviation from trends of tobacco yields, acreage, and quantities have been in the same overall range as those for the other commodities. The variation in tobacco price has been very much lower than the price variation for the other commodities. Over the period considered, the tobacco industry operated under a remarkably stable support price formula that linked nominal support price changes directly to the movement in an index of prices paid by farmers. (Calculations based on deviations from one-step-ahead ARIMA forecasts provide similar conclusions.)

Table 2 provides some information about the recent patterns of variability related to two tobacco types. The first four columns refer to fifty-four counties that produce flue-cured tobacco in North Carolina. These counties represent all four North Carolina flue-cured types, 11A, 11B, 12, and 13, and are representative of the whole flue-cured tobacco industry in terms of cultural practices, weather and terrain. Columns (1) and (2) are based on averages for the fifty-four counties.

TABLE 1. Variability in Tobacco and Other Major U.S. Commodities[a]

	Corn	Cotton	Wheat	Soybeans	Tobacco
Yield	11.6	11.8	8.1	6.7	9.1
Acreage	11.2	19.1	14.0	8.2	11.7
Quantity	14.2	19.9	11.3	13.0	11.5
Deflated price	20.7	21.5	26.5	19.8	3.9

Source: Adapted from data in Sumner and Alston (1986), chapter 7.

[a]Table entries are the standard deviations of residuals from a
regression of the log of the variable on time. They may be
interpreted as the average percentage deviations from the logarithmic
trend line. Data are from USDA sources and cover the years 1950
through 1983.

TABLE 2. Recent Variability in the Maryland and North Carolina Flue-Cured Tobacco Industries, 1977-1984

	Flue-Cured[a]				Maryland[b]
	State Level		County Level		Whole Industry
Variable	$(1)^c$	$(2)^d$	$(3)^c$	$(4)^d$	$(5)^c$
	(percent)				
Yield	6.8	5.7	9.4	8.0	4.0
Acres	15.7	6.9	17.7	8.8	18.5
Production	15.2	11.2	19.0	14.2	22.5
Basic quota	11.4	4.6	11.9	5.4	
Effective quota	13.4	6.1	16.2	8.1	
Support price[e]	4.1	2.7	4.1	2.7	
Market price[e]	4.8	4.6	5.4	5.1	17.0
Quota lease rate[e]	11.9	8.5	19.3	12.0	
Total revenue	16.7	11.5	20.3	14.3	20.9
Lease income	10.7	4.1	18.6	14.1	
Marginal cost	8.7	4.0	9.2	4.7	

Source: Calculations based on data from Tobacco Situation and Outlook Report (1986) and a North Carolina State University survey of county agents.

[a]The flue-cured tobacco entries are calculated from fifty-four North Carolina counties from across the state in Types 11A, 11B, 12, and 13.
[b]This refers to national figures for type 32.
[c]These table entries are coefficients of variation. For column (3) they are the mean of the coefficients of variation for the fifty-four counties.
[d]These are standard deviations of residuals from linear trends divided by the mean of the data. For column (4) they are the mean of standard deviations divided by the sample mean.
[e]The prices, incomes and cost are deflated using the prices paid index.

Over the recent period of 1977 to 1984 average yields were relatively stable while acreage was falling in line with basic quota levels. Production has been more variable than either of its components when considered as deviation from trend. The support price and market price were quite stable with little real trend. The quota lease rate has been more variable than prices and also more variable than marginal costs, which are defined as price minus lease rate. At the state level average lease income, defined as lease rate times effective quota, has been more stable than either of its two components. Quota and lease rate tend to move in opposite directions because a reduction in quota drives lease prices up. Total revenue has been more variable than either its price or its quantity component, but very similar to the variability of production. This suggests low negative covariance of price and quantity.

The second two columns in Table 2 are based on variability at the county level. Column (3) reports averages of coefficients of variation calculated for the data from each county, whereas column (4) reports averages of the standard deviations of residuals from linear trends for each county relative to the means. These columns provide a measure of year-to-year variability as observed in the county markets. For local economies and agribusiness firms, county variation in acres and output is more relevant than the variation at the state or national level.

Because intercounty movement of quota is not allowed, county-level variation in lease rates is also important. Comparisons of columns (1) to (3) and (2) to (4) in Table 2 show that lease rates, effective quota, and lease incomes are all considerably more variable at the county level than at the aggregate level. Yields, acres, production, price, and total revenues are all somewhat more variable at the county level. It is useful to note that some county markets have experienced much less or much more stable conditions. The coefficient of variation calculated for each county for acres, effective quota, production, and total revenue all ranged from about 12 percent to around 30 percent. Measures of lease rate and lease income variability were spread even more widely across the counties.

Individual farmers are affected by individual variability, not state or average county-level variability. Farmers face similar levels of support price or basic quota variation. Actual market price depends on the specific qualities produced, auction market chosen, and the days that the farmer sells his crop. Effective quota also depends on

farm-specific patterns of past yields, and farms may have
quite different patterns of yields.

Recent evidence from Kentucky provides some evidence on
the amount of individual farm yield variability relative to
county averages. For the crop years 1974 to 1982, Debrah
and Hall (1987) reported coefficients of variation of county
average yields of 10 percent for burley tobacco and 12.4
percent for corn. At the individual farm level they found
coefficients of variation of yields of 24.7 percent for
burley tobacco and 16.6 percent for corn. The county
average data they report are similar to the county-level
yield variability reported in Table 2 for flue-cured
tobacco. If flue-cured tobacco is between burley tobacco
and corn in the ratio of individual to county coefficient of
variation, we may expect individual producers of flue-cured
tobacco to face coefficients of variation of yield of close
to 20 percent. Individual farm variability of total revenue
is probably much higher than the 20 percent indicated for
the county level in Table 2. This is due partly to less
negative correlation between individual farm yields and
market price.

The final column of Table 2 provides evidence on
variability in the Maryland tobacco industry. The Maryland
tobacco industry has been essentially unregulated for many
years. About half the crop is exported and the rest is used
in U.S. cigarettes. Given its potential substitutability
with flue-cured and burley types, the demand for Maryland
tobacco would be expected to be relatively elastic. In 1981
some Maryland-type tobacco was grown in North Carolina, and
production jumped by 80 percent in that year. In subsequent
years, production of Maryland tobacco was restricted by law
to those areas that did not have quota or allotment for
other types. (Some of the crop is grown in Pennsylvania.)

About 25 to 30 million pounds of Maryland tobacco is
produced. This is less than one-twentieth of the national
output of flue-cured tobacco and less than the amount of
tobacco produced in many North Carolina counties.

Comparing column (5) with columns (1) and (3) shows
that Maryland tobacco yields were less variable than
flue-cured yields over the 1977-1984 period. Acres and
production were slightly more variable than the average for
North Carolina counties. The market price for Maryland
tobacco has been much more variable than the price for
flue-cured tobacco. The Maryland price fell in real terms
in the early 1980s, whereas the flue-cured price was held
relatively high until the large drop in real net price to
growers starting with the 1985 crop. The low flue-cured

prices since 1985 are not included in this sample. The
Maryland price in 1983 was very low because the drought
affected average quality.

Total revenue in the Maryland industry is only slightly
more variable than for the average North Carolina county.
Overall, in comparison with the Maryland industry the
flue-cured program seems to have smoothed out the output
price but has not reduced output or total revenue
variability to a major extent.

RISK AND QUOTA OWNERSHIP

Tobacco quota is a valuable asset that was created by
the tobacco program. Before 1982 quota could not be sold
independently of the farm to which it was assigned. In
recent years explicit sales of quota have allowed analysts
to measure a direct price of quota for each county market.
This quota price varies from county to county and depends on
expectations of future market conditions. The one-year
lease rate for one pound of quota depends on the difference
between the anticipated market price of tobacco for the next
year and the marginal cost of producing that pound of
tobacco. Ownership of quota allows one the valuable right
to sell tobacco into the future. The amount of future sales
associated with a pound of quota depends on the national
effective quota of that type of tobacco in future years. As
total quota falls or rises, the right to sell for each unit
of quota declines or increases proportionately. For
example, 1,000 pounds of flue-cured quota purchased in 1982
would have allowed the sale of slightly over 700 pounds in
1986. The capital value of quota depends on the anticipated
amount of national quota in all future years and the amount
by which anticipated market price exceeds anticipated
marginal cost. These depend on underlying supply and demand
conditions, the political economy of price supports and
quotas and the continued existence of the program.
Capitalization also depends on the interest rate.

The relationship of the annual lease rate for tobacco
quota to the sales price of quota provides information about
market participants' expectations of tobacco prices and
quota levels. The higher ratio of lease rate to sales
price, the lower the expected prices or quantities in future
years. Based on the conditions discussed above, the sales
price for a unit of effective quota sold in year zero may be
written as:

$$S_0 = \sum_{t=0}^{\infty} \frac{L_t k_t \rho_t}{(1+r)^t}$$

where L_t is the expected lease rate for quota, k_t is the relative amount of effective quota in year t compared to the amount purchased in year 0 ($k_0=1$), ρ_t is the probability that the program will be in force in year t ($\rho_0 = 1$), and r is the appropriate interest rate.

Using a relatively high rate of return of 10 percent and assuming that prices and quotas were expected to remain stable over the whole future, the price of quota will be ten times the annual lease. As an example, in 1984 the lease rate in South Carolina averaged about $0.50 per pound, so using $k = \rho = 1$ and $r = 0.1$ quota would sell for $5.00/pound. Factors that reduce expected lease rates, reduce expected quota levels, or reduce the expected probability of continued existence of the program reduce the sales price. In 1984 the average price of quota in South Carolina was $1.63 (Dangerfield and Thompson, 1987; and Dangerfield, Thompson, and Loyd, 1987).

Clearly, participants in the South Carolina quota market exhibited a high degree of pessimism about the future value of quota. They were right; changes did occur. In the following three years after 1984 the price of tobacco (net of rebates to buyers) has been about 25 cents per pound below 1984 levels, and the quantity of quota has averaged about 90 percent of the 1984 amount. The average lease value for quota has been about 60 percent of the 1984 level, so lease income is only 54 percent of what it was in 1984. A pound purchased in the spring of 1984 will have returned about $1.30 by the end of 1987 in discounted implied lease income (using $r = 0.10$). It will take at least two more years to have "paid off" the initial investment.

Table 3 provides evidence of quota lease rates and sales price from counties in North Carolina. The price of quota fell in each year in all growing areas. For 1983 and 1984 sales price fell even though lease rates rose. This indicated an increase in the expectation that future prices or quantities would decline or that the program would end (thus causing a fall to zero in quota lease rate). In 1985 the lease rates and sales prices fell by an average of about 40 percent. The ratio of sales price to lease rate rose slightly.

We have no evidence of the price of quota or lease rate for 1986. However, the program changes that were made final in that year seemed to make the program more secure and

TABLE 3. North Carolina Flue-Cured Tobacco Quota Lease Rates and Sales Prices, by Type

	Year			
	1982	1983	1984	1985
	($ per pound)			

Type 11 - Piedmont, old and middle belts

	1982	1983	1984	1985
Lease rate	0.41	0.46	0.48	0.27
Sales price	2.52	2.23	1.90	1.26
Sales/lease	6.1	4.8	4.0	4.7

Type 12 - Coastal plain, eastern belt

	1982	1983	1984	1985
Lease rate	0.49	0.57	0.59	0.34
Sales price	3.10	2.86	2.47	1.31
Sales/lease	6.3	5.0	4.2	3.9

Type 13 - Southern coastal plain, border belt

	1982	1983	1984	1985
Lease rate	0.52	0.53	0.56	0.36
Sales price	2.69	2.53	2.07	1.69
Sales/lease	5.2	4.8	3.7	4.7

State average

	1982	1983	1984	1985
Lease rate	0.46	0.52	0.55	0.32
Sales price	2.86	2.58	2.21	1.34
Sales/lease	6.2	5.0	4.0	4.2

Source: Calculations based on data from a North Carolina State University survey of county agents.

would have tended to raise sales price of quota. The end of quota leasing in 1987 would tend to shift out both the supply and demand for quota in the sales market. The percent of quota leased out fell in each year from 1982 to 1985.

Overall, the sales price of quota is severely discounted relative to current income flow because of potential program changes. Restrictions that buyers of quota must be active tobacco producers also means that returns on investments in quota will be highly correlated with the returns to the farming activity. Elimination of lease and transfer eliminates an opportunity for tobacco growers and quota owners to diversify their portfolios and may make tobacco production significantly more risky.

CONCLUSION

Does the tobacco program make investment in the tobacco industry less risky? Let us first consider the affirmative answer. In the spring of 1987, for a grower leasing quota, renting land, and making other preparations for the 1987 crop, the program allows him to be confident of the price he will receive for his crop this fall. That price will average about $1.50 per pound, give or take a few cents.

If there were no tobacco program, the grower would make his 1987 investments with less confidence about the 1987 price. Depending on overall yields and quality and depending on supplies from other countries, the price this fall could range over a relatively wide margin. This range of prices is bounded mostly by the low cost of storage of tobacco relative to its price.

Now, consider 1988 and beyond. Farmers and others in the industry are not in the business for a single year. Investments are made with a view to the longer-run prospects for the industry. Evidence from the sales market for quota suggests that producers, lenders, or other agribusiness firms making long-term investments recognize that the program provides little assurance about the industry, say, five years from now. If the demand for U.S. leaf falls, the program enforces a fall in U.S. price and U.S. quantity. The program will smooth out year-to-year price movements, but these will be replaced in part with quantity fluctuations and with fluctuations in the value of quota. But more important, the tobacco program simply cannot shield the industry from the consequences of long-term changes in demand conditions.

If an investor thinks that there is a significant chance that there will be a decline in the long-term demand for U.S. leaf, the existence of the tobacco program does little to make his investment more secure. In fact, the program may make long-term investments significantly more risky. In addition to the risk implied by underlying demand and cost conditions, investors now face the chance that the tobacco program may be changed.

In terms of its effects on stability, then, the tobacco program may be viewed partly as a tradeoff between less unanticipated year-to-year variability in output price for less individual control over year-to-year output changes, more variability in input (quota) costs, and more uncertainty about long-term returns to investments.

APPENDIX

A Simple Model

This appendix uses a few simple equations to characterize the model of the tobacco market illustrated in Figure 1. The underlying cost and demand relationships are represented algebraically and then the operation of the tobacco program is contrasted with the results of a free market. I solve for equations that indicate the determinants of variability of tobacco prices, quantities, costs and revenues both with and without the tobacco program.

To keep the model manageable, I will assume each equation is linear and is as simple as possible. Beginning on the supply side of the market, anticipated marginal cost of production, m_t^a depends on anticipated output:

$$m_t^a = \beta_t^a + \mu Q_t^a \tag{1}$$

where the intercept β^a (which is allowed to change from year to year but is known at the beginning of the crop year) and the slope parameter, μ, are both positive. Actual quantity produced depends on anticipated quantity and a random factor that represents mostly weather-induced variation from normal yields:

$$Q_t = Q_t^a + y_t. \tag{2}$$

On the demand side of the market, we again separate anticipations and realizations. At the beginning of the crop year, anticipated demand, D_t^a, depends on the anticipated price, P_t^a:

$$D_t^a = \alpha_t^a - \eta P_t^a , \tag{3}$$

where α_t^a may change from year to year but is known at the beginning of the year and both α_t^a and η are positive. Actual market price depends on the actual realized quantity. This may be indicated

$$P_t - P_t^a = -\gamma y_t, \tag{4}$$

where γ is positive, so the deviation of realized price, P_t, from the anticipated price for the year depends inversely on deviations of realized quantity from anticipated quantity. Equation (4) is a short-run demand function in price dependent form that represents demand due to storage and other short-run adjustments made after the harvest is known.

Now we can use equations (1) through (4) to solve for the reduced-form expressions for the tobacco price and quantity. To do this requires the appropriate equilibrium conditions, and these, in turn, depend on whether the tobacco program is in place. First, consider equilibrium in the market without the program. Setting marginal cost equal to price and substituting equation (1) into equation (3) yields

$$D_t^a = \alpha_t^a - \eta(\beta_t^a + \mu Q_t^a).$$

Using the condition that quantity demanded equals quantity supplied, $D_t^a = Q_t^a$, and using Q_t^a to denote that quantity, leaves us with:

$$Q_t^a = [1/(1+\eta\mu)](\alpha_t^a - \eta\beta_t^a) \ . \tag{5}$$

Substituting into (2) gives us a reduced-form output expression:

$$Q_t = [1/(1+\eta\mu)](\alpha_t^a - \eta\beta_t^a) + y_t . \tag{6}$$

The price equations are solved similarly:

$$P_t^a = [1/(1+\eta\mu)](\mu\alpha_t^a + \beta_t^a) \tag{7}$$

and

$$P_t = [1/(1+\eta\mu)](\mu\alpha_t^a + \beta_t^a) - \gamma y_t . \tag{8}$$

The equilibrium condition with the tobacco program in place is different. Prior to 1982 the support price depended on a formula that included a base price and adjustments in an index of prices paid by farmers. Between 1982 and 1986 the price and the grower assessments to fund the program were determined year by year by ad hoc legislation and administrative decisions. Following the 1986 law, changes in the support price depend on a weighted average of past price movements and an index of production costs with some administrative discretion. But the relevant effective price nets out an assessment per pound paid to finance the program. This assessment is determined by the USDA. For simplicity we will simply take the anticipated price, P_t^a, under the program to be exogenously determined by the regulators. Note that P_t^a is not equal to the support price but is above the support price net of assessment by some amount that reflects normal market conditions.

With the anticipated price set exogenously, the USDA sets the quota based on anticipated demand. This relationship is represented by equation (3). So final output is given in reduced form by:

$$Q_t = \alpha_t^a - \eta P_t^a + y_t \tag{9}$$

and price by

$$P_t = P_t^a - \gamma y_t \tag{10}$$

where P_t^a is exogenous.

The framework laid out here has assumed that the tobacco program does not affect the underlying parameters of supply and demand that determine price and quantity responses. These parameters, indicated by Greek letters, will be mostly invariant to the regulation in so long as the program does not change the basic incentives to produce and use tobacco.

Under the tobacco program the variability in price and quantity depend on variation in the support price which directly determines the variation in P_t^a. Using the variance as our measure of variability and Var P_g^a to denote the variance of the anticipated price with a government program, we get the following expressions for the price and quantity variances:

$$\text{Var } Q_g = \text{Var } \alpha^a + \eta^2 \text{Var}(P_g^a) + \text{Var}(y) \tag{9'}$$

$$\text{Var } P_g = \text{Var } (P_g^a) + \gamma^2 \text{Var}(y). \tag{10'}$$

I have assumed that variations in the parameter α, the government set price, and yields are each independent of the others.

Without the tobacco program, free market quantity and price variances are:

$$\text{Var } Q_f = [1/(1+\eta\mu)]^2 \text{Var}(\alpha^a)$$
$$+ [(\eta/(1+\eta\mu))]^2 \text{Var}(\beta^a) + \text{Var}(y) \text{ and,} \tag{6'}$$

$$\text{Var } P_f = [\mu/(1+\eta\mu)]^2 \text{ Var}(\alpha^a)$$

$$+ [1/(1+\eta\mu]^2 \text{ Var}(\beta^a) + \gamma^2 \text{ Var}(y). \tag{8'}$$

A comparison of (8') with (10') makes clear that if P^a_g is kept stable, the price of tobacco can be held relatively stable. This is especially true given that the parameter γ is the inverse of a short-run demand responsiveness and will be small given the potential to store tobacco if the crop is large.

With no tobacco program the reduced expression for total cost is:

$$C_t = \psi + \theta(1-\mu\eta\theta)\alpha_t\beta_t + 1/2\mu\theta^2\alpha_t^2 + \theta\eta((1/2)\mu\theta\eta-1)\beta_t^2 \tag{11}$$

where ψ is a constant and $\theta = (1/1+\eta\mu)$ and the superscript, a, has been suppressed. Total revenue, P_tQ_t is:

$$R_t = \theta^2(1-\mu\eta)\alpha_t\beta_t + \theta^2\mu\alpha_t^2 - \theta^2\eta\beta_t^2$$

$$+ \theta(\mu - c)\alpha_ty_t + \theta(+ \gamma\eta)\beta_ty_t - \gamma y_t^2 . \tag{12}$$

Net revenue is simply $R_t - C_t$ and will not be written out here.

With the tobacco program in place, the reduced form expressions depend on P^a_t:

$$C_t = \psi + \alpha_t\beta_t - \eta\beta_tP^a_t + (1/2)\mu\alpha_t^2 - \mu\eta P^a_t$$

$$+ (1/2)\mu\eta^2(P^a_t)^2 \tag{13}$$

and

$$R_t = \alpha_tP^a_t - \gamma\alpha_ty_t - \eta(P^a_t)^2$$

$$+ (\eta\gamma+1)P^a_t\, y_t - \gamma y_t^2 . \tag{14}$$

136

The tobacco program creates the implicit or explicit market to lease tobacco quota. The lease rate per pound of quota is equal to the difference between the market price and marginal cost. This varies by county and in reduced form is:

$$L_t^a = \mu\alpha_t - \beta_t + (1+\mu\eta)P_t^a. \tag{15}$$

The amount paid for quota is the lease rate times the amount of quota.

$$L_t^a Q_t^a = -\mu\alpha_t^2 - \beta_t\alpha_t + (1+2\mu\eta)P_t^a\alpha_t$$
$$- \eta\beta_t P_t^a - (1+\mu\eta)\eta(P_t^a)^2. \tag{16}$$

A complete analysis of the variability facing the tobacco industry requires consideration of the variances of these costs and revenues as well as output price and quantity. Derivation of these variances is straightforward, but the expressions are ugly and will not be presented here.

REFERENCES

Debrah, Siegfried H. and Harry H. Hall. "County Data Versus Individual-Farm Data for Measuring Crop-Yield Variability." Department of Agricultural Economics Staff Paper No. 214, University of Kentucky, January 1987.

Dangerfield, Coleman W., Jr. and C. Stassen Thompson. "The Market for Flue-Cured Tobacco Production Rights." Paper presented at the winter meetings of the Southern Agricultural Economics Association, Nashville, TN, January 31-February 4, 1987.

Dangerfield, Coleman W., Jr., C. Stassen Thompson, and Max I. Loyd. "Program Uncertainty and the Market for Flue-Cured Tobacco Quota in South Carolina Since the 1982 Act." Paper presented at the 32nd Tobacco Workers Conference, Baltimore, MD, January 12-15, 1987.

Goodwin, Barry, Daniel A. Sumner, and D. Arthur Sparrow. "Identification and Estimation of Underlying Market Supply Function Parameters for a Commodity with Mandatory Output Controls." Presented at the 1987 annual meetings of the AAEA, August 1987. Department of Economics and Business, N. C. State University, Box 8110, Raleigh, NC, 27695.

Grise, Verner. "Effects of Terminating Lease and Transfer of Flue-Cured Tobacco Quotas and Allotments." Draft. Washington, D.C.: U.S. Department of Agriculture, Economic Research Service, National Economic Division, 1986.

Johnson, D. Gale. Forward Prices for Agriculture. New York: Arno Press, 1976.

Loyd, Max I. "Tobacco Marketing Alternatives." In Tobacco Marketing Policy Alternatives. Southern Extension Marketing Publication 79-1, Leaflet 6, North Carolina Agricultural Extension Service, September 1979.

Marshall, J. Paxton, Max I. Loyd, and D. Milton Shuffett. "Fundamental Changes in U.S. Government Tobacco Programs--And Some Unfinished Work." Paper presented at the 32nd Tobacco Workers Conference, Baltimore, MD, January 12-15, 1987.

Schultz, Theodore W. The Economic Organization of Agriculture. New York: McGraw-Hill, 1953.

Sumner, Daniel A., and Julian M. Alston. Effects of the Tobacco Program: An Analysis of Deregulation. Washington, D.C.: American Enterprise Institute for Public Policy Research, 1986.

----------. "Substitutability for Farm Commodities: The Demand for U.S. Tobacco in Cigarette Manufacturing." American Journal of Agricultural Economics 69(1987):258-265.

Tweeten, Luther. "Economic Instability in Agriculture: The Contributions of Prices, Government Programs and Exports." American Journal of Agricultural Economics 65(1983):922-931.

U.S. Department of Agriculture. Tobacco Situation and Outlook Report. Washington, D.C.: U.S. Department of Agriculture, Economic Research Service, June 1986 and September 1987.

Reaction

Max I. Loyd

Dr. Sumner has done an outstanding job in laying the groundwork for analyzing price instability in the tobacco industry. His paper includes a concise, simplified, but theoretically sound discussion of the economic losses resulting from price instability--particularly price variation caused by unanticipated changes in market conditions. The paper more than met the requirement in the context of this symposium.

Dr. Sumner's model was not intended to provide a complete description of the industry. It is to be used as a reference point in discussing the impact of, and adjustments to, shifts in supply and demand. The model serves this purpose well.

Both the supply of and the demand for tobacco appear to be considerably more elastic than for other major commodities, based on the best available research results. This means, as the paper asserts, that adjustments to variation in supply and demand schedules generally would be more in quantity adjustments than in prices. As co-author of one of the references cited, I should point out that some previous generalizations based on pre-program history (when supply and demand were less elastic) overstate potential price variability in the industry.

Dr. Sumner concludes that "the [tobacco] program may make long-term investments significantly more risky." The values shown in his Tables 2 and 3 generally support this conclusion. As pointed out, "overall, in comparison to the Maryland industry the flue-cured program seems to have

Professor, Department of Agricultural Economics and Rural Sociology, Clemson University.

smoothed out the output price but has not reduced output or total revenue variability to a major extent." Furthermore, with the program, producers have to deal with the risk associated with the variation in quota lease rates or in quota sales prices (Tables 2, 3). Sumner points out that the program simply cannot shield the industry from the consequences of long-term changes in demand conditions. This is particularly true for tobacco because of the no-net cost provision. That is, a decline in demand for tobacco would require some combination of lower support prices, lower quota, and/or increased program cost for producers.

Producers apparently prefer the current program, even with its recent substantive changes, to no program at all. In the April 1986 referendum, the vote was 93.7 percent in favor of the program. This preference could exist partly because producers can put some limit on the amount of quota-associated risk that they are willing and able to take. Producers also apparently feel that the potential for price variability is greater than Sumner's analysis indicates. They have no modern experience with an unregulated market, except for minor non-program types such as Maryland tobacco. Grower expectations about price variation are likely influenced by conditions that existed prior to the 1930s and by observation of other commodity prices.

As the paper states, more research is needed on price/quantity/revenue behavior in the industry. I would caution against heavy reliance on experience with Maryland tobacco. The short-term demand for Maryland tobacco is likely to be more elastic than that for flue-cured and burley. This is because Maryland tobacco can be substituted for the major types within a considerable range. The average percentage of Maryland tobacco in U.S. cigarette blends has ranged from 1.3 to 2.6 percent since 1977. (The only feasible substitutes for flue-cured and burley are foreign tobaccos of the same type. The short-term range of substitution is relatively limited.)

I would also suggest that three of the areas discussed in the paper be considered further in evaluations of the potential for tobacco price variation. First, supply may be less elastic in the short run than the paper implies. The intermediate-run estimate of greater than 4 might be valid, but a short-run elasticity would be more appropriate in estimating year-to-year price variation. (As the paper suggests, producers might learn to live with year-to-year fluctuations if the mid-term path were relatively smooth or predictable. But year-to-year fluctuations might complicate price prediction and in any case are of major concern to producers.) The elasticity estimate relies heavily on the elasticity of factor supply. Land is discussed as an example, and the generalization is valid. However, tobacco-specific equipment and facilities are a much more important input than land. These account for about 15 percent of total production costs for flue-cured and about 20 percent for burley. In a declining market these assets remain in use as long as they are expected to receive any positive return, thus limiting supply adjustments. In a rising market, expansion beyond existing capacity would not occur until expected returns exceeded total costs, including risk. (The U.S. tobacco industry currently has excess capacity--which of course reflects earlier risky decisions.) Thus, supply adjustments alone would permit substantial price variation.

Another area that needs more consideration is the storage function. Storage demand will depend more on price expectations versus the nominal interest rate than on physical storage costs. The paper contrasts tobacco and wheat, where annual physical storage costs are only about .25 percent of the market price for tobacco versus about 10 percent of the market price for wheat. Cotton could be used as a current example to question the effect of physical storage costs versus price expectations. Annual physical costs for storing cotton amount to about 4 to 5 percent of the current price. Spot cotton prices dropped more than 60 percent last fall but have recently rebounded to about the previous level. Admittedly, this range of prices could not have occurred without a change in the cotton program. However, this amount of variation would not have occurred in any case if physical storage costs were the major determinant of storage decisions.

Finally, short-run price behavior for tobacco might be affected by the dominance of a small number of buyers. Two firms buy about 60 percent of the flue-cured tobacco that is used domestically. (A substantial part of this tobacco is bought on order through dealers but the effect is still the same generally.) This may not be a problem for grades/qualities of tobacco that are also bought for export. However, the export buyers do not even bid on certain grades that normally represent nearly half the crop. (The non-export grades generally are related to stalk position but other quality factors apply.) One could argue that any influence of imperfect competition is built into the demand equation and is reflected in estimates of the elasticity of demand. The opposing argument is that we cannot accurately model the influence of imperfect competition and that it is reflected as part of the unexplained price variation.

For too long, attitudes toward tobacco price stabilization measures have been based on guesswork--or on poor logic, using questionable assumptions. Sumner's paper and his previous work are major contributions to an improved approach. The above suggestions are offered for consideration in further research on this topic. Sumner's paper is commendable in the background that it provides and in its challenge for further research.

6

Stability Issues
and Policy Analysis

Gordon C. Rausser

ABSTRACT

The themes in this paper are basically three; each theme relates to a different cause of instability within the agriculture sector. All of these sources of instability beg for additional conceptual and empirical work. The first source of instability will be defined as internal, the second as external or multimarket, and the third and as public policies. It is argued that a comprehensive view of instability and uncertainty in the agricultural sector of the United States or in other countries cannot be achieved without acknowledging the contributions of all three major sources of instability.

The first major issue in agricultural sector stability analysis is how large are the potential benefits from correcting whatever market failures exist? The second major issue relates to the potential failures in governmental implementation. Are the costs associated with these failures sufficiently "small" to justify public policy correction of particular market failures in agriculture?

A major reason why a more comprehensive set of risk markets has not arisen within the private sector can be traced directly to heavy governmental intervention. So much of the risk is borne or is potentially borne by the public sector that little incentive exists for the emergence of private institutions to manage inherent instabilities and risks.

A potentially far more important set of issues than those outlined above relates to the longer-term unstable economic waves that have been observed for the U.S. agricultural sector. If the U.S. agricultural

Robert Gordon Sproul Chair Professor, Department of Agricultural and Resource Economics, University of California, Berkeley; and Special Consultant, Council of Economic Advisers, Washington, D.C.

sector were only faced with short-term instabilities, the recent
crisis would not have arisen. It is far easier to design effective
institutions for managing short-term than long-term instabilities.

INTRODUCTION

The instability and riskiness of agriculture has long
been recognized. In his seminal piece on U.S. agriculture,
Schultz (1945) argued:

> Farm prices change more frequently and fluctuate
> more widely than any other set of producer
> prices. Constantly changing prices have their
> cost, usually resulting in waste and costly
> maladjustments....Farm prices in the past,
> altogether too erratic, have not only burdened
> agriculture with much unnecessary price
> uncertainty, but their instability has impaired
> appreciably the positive functioning of prices,
> namely, to guide and direct production. (p. 42)

Acceptance of this view is reflected in many of our
current institutions. For example, the exemptions allowed
agriculture under the General Agreement on Tariffs and Trade
(GATT) originally were justified by the risk and instability
within agriculture as compared to that in manufacturing
sectors. The United States can claim responsibility for the
initial exemptions in Article 11 of GATT. Because of these
exemptions, multilateral trade negotiations have failed,
time and again, to bring agricultural trade under any set of
consistent, liberal rules. As a result, the original
justification for agricultural exemptions ironically has led
to the current disorder and instability in international
agricultural markets.

In addition to internal sources of instability outlined
by Schultz and others (see Blandford and Currie, 1975),
evidence has begun to accumulate on external market sources
of instability (Andrews and Rausser, 1986; Rausser et al.,
1986). Macroeconomic phenomena, especially interest rates
and exchange rates, have been hypothesized to be a major
source of instability within the agricultural sector. To
the extent that this instability is explained by the
fixed-price/flex-price disequilibrium specification, another
potential market failure justification is offered for
governmental intervention.

Market failures, internal or external, do not explain
(normatively or positively) governmental intervention.

Gardner (1983, 1987) has argued that U.S. government commodity programs essentially are income redistribution mechanisms. In the Gardner analysis, however, no market failures exist and thus the competitive equilibrium is a Pareto optimum. In this setting governmental intervention plays no role in correcting market failures or lowering transactions costs (a political economic resource transaction (PERT) governmental intervention) and thus indirectly increasing societal welfare. This perspective presumes that governmental intervention comes in the form of political economic-seeking transfers (PESTs) (Rausser, 1982). PESTs are all those rent-seeking activities by individual groups which distort public policies and lead to government or political failure. The literature on government failure has made it clear that public policy not only absorbs some risks within the private sector, but also can become another source of instability and uncertainty. Political-economic markets, with their role in endogenous government behavior, require policy instabilities and risks to be assessed along with market instabilities and risks.

Focusing on issues of stability in terms of what is rather than what ought to be, the themes of this paper are basically three. Each theme relates to a different source of instability within the agriculture sector; all of these sources beg for additional conceptual and empirical work. The first source of instability will be defined as internal, the second source as external or multimarket, and the third and final source of instability as public policies. It is argued that a comprehensive view of instability and uncertainty within the agricultural sector of the United States or other countries cannot be achieved without acknowledging the contribution of all three major sources of instability.

INTERNAL INSTABILITY AND INCOMPLETE MARKETS

Prior to the early 1970s, the common explanations for internal instability within U.S. agriculture were (1) on the demand side, the inelastic nature of aggregate food demand and the low-income elasticity of demand; and (2) on the supply side, weather patterns, rapid technological change, atomistic behavior, and asset fixity (Hathaway, 1963). The inherent instability resulting from these characteristics-- without governmental intervention--was regarded as undesirable by many of those involved in the food and agricultural system (from input suppliers to producers, assemblers, processors, distributors and consumers). The same stance is taken in the recent papers prepared by the Organization for Economic Cooperation and Development (OECD) Working Party I. Even though this working party argues strongly for liberalization and major reforms of agricultural policies through the developed world of OECD, they nevertheless accept the view that internal instability within agricultural sectors is undesirable to society as a whole.

The inherent instability and uncertainty within the agricultural sector by itself is not sufficient justification for governmental intervention. Only if instability and excessive uncertainty are combined with an incomplete set of risk markets does a market failure justification for governmental intervention in U.S. agriculture exist. The inflexibility of some assets employed within the sector is another potential justification for governmental intervention. Still another potential explanation is noncompetitive behavior within the vertical marketing chain for agricultural products.

Incomplete Markets

Incomplete markets arise because of high transaction costs and various types of imperfect information. These include asymmetric information, moral hazard, adverse selection, and principal/agent problems (Ross, 1973). Both static and dynamic models have been designed to represent these problems. In adverse selection models, information may be conveyed either by examination or by self-selection. The action which conveys information may be quantity-related or price-related; in some cases it is not the action of a single individual which conveys information but the action of groups of individuals. In these models, it makes a difference whether the uninformed individual moves first or whether the informed individual moves first (for example, individuals must purchase a level of education before employers will make job offers).

Private insurance markets face serious obstacles in agriculture, for reasons of both adverse selection and moral hazard. That is, a farmer is likely to be better informed about the hazards he faces than the insurer (adverse selection), and there are actions the farmer can take to affect output (moral hazard). In essence, although the farmer cannot affect whether there is a hailstorm, he can affect the losses he incurs by taking precautions.

Most models to date have been characterized by one-sided imperfect information; e.g., the borrower knows the characteristics of the lender, but the lender does not know the characteristics of the borrower (Bester, 1985). In some research, models with two-sided imperfect information have been specified. Though only a few general principles apply to all markets, some natural parameterizations and simplifications seem more appropriate in some markets, while others seem more appropriate in other markets (Fama and Jensen, 1983; Innes, 1986).

Economists have been able to demonstrate that incomplete markets and asymmetric information are closely linked. With complete markets, a farmer can sell the set of state-contingent commodity bundles he produces, thereby internalizing the cost and benefits of any actions he takes. However, if other agents cannot distinguish the effects of states and actions, contracts can only be made contingent on an observable variable and markets cannot be state-contingent--or, therefore, complete. Thus, asymmetric information is associated with the incomplete market inefficiencies and with "incomplete" contract forms. These contract forms give rise to a second source of inefficiency: the action-choosing agent (e.g., the farmer) does not consider the costs/benefits to be incurred/ enjoyed by other parties to a contract, and an externality is present (Greenwald and Stiglitz, 1986).

The lack of a complete set of contingency markets dramatically alters the implications of standard welfare economics (Rausser, 1982; Innes and Rausser, 1986). This is formally demonstrated in the appendix to this paper. It is shown in the appendix that it is possible to design a simple model of incomplete markets that reverses the outcome of standard welfare analysis. In the model specified in the appendix, deficiency payments do not result in deadweight losses. Moreover, production controls are shown under certain conditions to be an optimal complementary policy to deficiency payments. In fact, for the incomplete markets specification of the appendix, the optimal deficiency-payment/production-control program can lead to a full Pareto optimum.

Private Stockholding and Market Instability

Recently, a number of justifications have been advanced for public stockholding (Newbery and Stiglitz, 1981; Schmitz, 1982). Long ago, Keynes (1938) argued that the inherent instability in commodity markets would lead to insufficient private stockholding. Risks associated with price volatility, uncertainty about the ultimate "normal price," and the length of time that stocks would have to be held were viewed as the three major factors for this result. Keynes argued, as did Houthakker some years later (1967), that government intervention was needed because of divergence between social and private risk. Bosworth and Lawrence (1982) consider this perspective along with a number of other justifications for government interventions to stabilize the prices of volatile commodities. They come to the conclusion that the divergence between social and private benefits provides the best justification for intervention. In particular, as argued in the section on public policy below, private stockholders will not store for extreme contingencies because they do not expect to receive the true scarcity value of their stocks during such periods.

Internal Inflexibility

Although much has been written about the asset fixity in the U.S. agricultural sector, it is of concern not so much with regard to physical capital as to human capital. As argued by Schultz (1945), "...the labor market in the non-agricultural sector is quantity rationed and thus inhibits the migration of labor from agriculture to industry." Moreover, many farmers expend great amounts of effort and capital in the production of cash income in order to at least cover the cash expenditures necessary to remain in farming. This is especially true for those farmers participating in the mid-size category of the trifurcated agricultural production sector.

Small farms, whose major source of income is off-farm employment, have some means for effectively managing the inherent riskiness and instability of farming. Asset fixity for these particular farmers is not a serious concern because of the opportunities for off-farm employment and the low transaction cost of moving from one type of employment to another. For larger farms with off-farm income generated from other assets, a more balanced portfolio provides an effective means for managing the inherent riskiness and instability of agricultural markets. Moreover, the human capital asset fixity for these larger operations is rather minimal. Human capital asset fixity is most important for mid-sized farms. Hence, as the relative portion of the mid-size farming operations (which have limited off-farm income opportunities) has fallen, the importance of human capital fixity has declined over time as a distinguishing characteristic of U.S. agriculture. Equivalently, this

outcome has occurred as farms have become more integrated
into the balance of the U.S. economy.

Noncompetitive Markets

Within the vertical marketing chain for agricultural
products, many intermediaries (assemblers, processors,
wholesalers, distributors, marketing boards, etc.) exist.
As shown by Bieri and Schmitz (1974), for noncompetitive
market structures, intermediaries or middlemen can benefit
by "manufacturing" instability. They demonstrate that
intermediaries who act as monopolists on the sell side and
as monopsonists on the buy side will maximize their profits
by stabilizing prices to buyers but destabilizing
procurement or grower prices. Even though an intermediary
stores a portion of the good produced, there is a clear
advantage to destabilizing producer prices while stabilizing
consumer prices. In this framework, if instability occurs
as a natural phenomenon, the intermediary simply gains from
storing, acting as a monopolist and as a monopsonist.
However, if instability is not caused by natural forces, the
framework suggests that it would actually pay an
intermediary with monopoly and monopsony power to
manufacture instability at the expense of the rest of
society. In empirical analysis for a number of commodity
systems, evidence has begun to accumulate that inventories
held by intermediaries contribute to the stickiness of
prices toward the consumer end of the chain while augmenting
instability at lower levels of the marketing chain (see
Wohlgenant's discussion comments in this volume).

MARKET LINKAGES AND EXTERNAL SOURCES OF INSTABILITY[1]

The path followed by agricultural commodity prices over
much of the 1970s and 1980s is largely duplicated by other
flexible price commodity markets, e.g., gold, silver,
platinum, copper, lumber, etc. Stocks also accumulated for
these commodities during the 1970s and early 1980s. This
suggests that internal market conditions within agriculture
and governmental policies are only a part of the explanation
for the behavior of agricultural commodity markets. The
search for a complete explanation leads to a multimarket
perspective, namely an investigation of external linkages
with other markets.

Since 1972, the conventional wisdom has placed
increasingly less emphasis on the inherent instability in
commodity markets and more emphasis on external linkages

with other markets. During this period, the deregulation of the credit and banking system resulted in greater exposure of agriculture to conditions in the domestic money markets. Also, because of the shift from fixed exchange rates to flexible rates, commodity markets have become more exposed to international money markets and real trade among countries. Moreover, the emergence during this period of a well-integrated international capital market meant that agriculture, through domestic money and exchange rate markets, has become increasingly more dependent on capital flows among countries.

The linkages of commodity markets with U.S. money markets is indeed pervasive. Since farming is extremely capital-intensive and debt-to-asset ratios have risen dramatically over the last 10 years, movements in real interest rates have a significant effect on the cost structure facing agricultural production. Stock-carrying in storable commodity systems is sensitive to changes in interest rates; for nonstorable commodities (for example, live cattle and live hogs), breeding stocks are interest-rate sensitive. These effects, combined with the influence of interest rates on the value of the dollar, press grain products from both the demand side (for example, export demand, domestic livestock grain demand, and stockholding demand) and the cost side. The especially sensitive nature of agriculture to interest rates suggests that this sector is vulnerable to monetary and fiscal policy changes. It has been argued that since 1972, but particularly since 1980, the instability in monetary and fiscal policy has contributed greatly to the instability of commodity markets.

Overshooting

There is ample evidence that the U.S. agricultural sector has become more closely related to the rest of the domestic and international economies. The instability in monetary and fiscal policies is thought to have imposed sizable shocks on commodity markets. This is especially true if agricultural commodity markets behave as "flex-price" while other markets behave as "fixed-price." This fixed/flex price specification is necessary but not sufficient for money nonneutrality to imply overshooting (Rausser, 1985). Overshooting combined with "myopic" expectations means that "macro externalities" will be imposed upon the agricultural sector (Rausser et al., 1986). Flex-price commodity markets and fixed-price nonagricultural output markets combined with "small" output responses mean that overshooting in agricultural sector markets will occur even if expectations are formed rationally. Such overshooting results from the spillover effects of monetary and fiscal policy on commodity markets.

Without governmental price supports, agricultural prices generally are more flexible than nonagricultural prices. This is true in part because (1) contracts for agricultural commodities tend to be written for shorter duration and (2) biological lags tend to cause agricultural supply to be unresponsive to price changes in the short run. However, if output can conceivably respond sufficiently to more than compensate for a short-run spike or fall in flexible prices, market overshooting will not necessarily be observed.[2]

Given a world of fixed- and flex-price markets, the driving force behind overshooting is the "real rate of interest" and arbitrage across markets. When real interest rates rise above (fall below) the long-run equilibrium rate of interest, pressure arises in the short run to drive flexible commodity prices downward (upward). In much of the 1970s, real interest rates were below their long-run equilibrium levels; for some periods in the 1980s, they were above their long-run equilibrium levels. In the case of interest rates facing the U.S. agricultural sector, the degree of disequilibrium was even more pronounced because of the organizational structure and the relative importance of the farm credit system. This organizational structure amplifies the disequilibrium and generates more overshooting than would otherwise result. In the farm credit system, the borrowers are, in fact, owners, and no dividends are paid to stockholders. As a result, during favorable periods, the only way of extracting any surpluses that might be generated by the system is through owners increasing their level of borrowing at interest rates that are below prevailing interest rates for the rest of the economy. During unfavorable periods, the opposite situation exists. Because of this phenomenon, interest rates charged within the farm credit system through much of the 1970s were dramatically below interest rates facing the rest of the economy; while during the 1980s, the opposite occurred. Hence, interest rate market disequilibriums are even more pronounced for the agricultural sector, and the associated overshooting and instability for the sector are amplified relative to the balance of the U.S. economy.

Empirical Evidence on Overshooting

Empirical evidence supports the view that output response is not sufficient to counter the tendency for prices to overshoot and that expectations are at best only "myopically" rational. Bordo (1980) has shown empirically that prices of raw goods respond more quickly to changes in money supply than do prices of manufactured goods. Andrews and Rausser (1986) have shown that during the large cyclical downturns of the early 1930s and the early 1980s, prices fell more and quantities fell less in the agricultural sector than in any of nine other sectors of the U.S. economy. Numerous studies (e.g., Cumby and Obstfeld, 1984) have shown that real interest rates vary significantly across countries, refuting the old view that real interest rates are constant. These results also suggest that the purchasing power parity assumption does not hold, even approximately. In other words, exchange rate changes do not offset changes in relative price levels.

Frankel and Hardouvelis' (1985) study on monetary surprises rejects the flex/flex specification in favor of the fixed/flex specification. Their empirical results suggest that when money supply turns out to be greater than expected, nominal interest rates tend to rise and the prices of basic commodities tend to fall. If the flex/flex specification were correct, then interest rates and commodity markets would either both rise (if the announcement were to cause the public to revise upward its expectation of future money growth) or else both fall (if the public were to revise downward its expectation of future money growth). The only hypothesis that explains the reactions in both the interest rate and commodity markets is that the increase in nominal interest is also an increase in the real interest rate. This is presumably because the public anticipates that the Federal Reserve will reverse the recent fluctuations in money stock, thus increasing interest rates and depressing the real prices of commodities.

In some work that is under way at Berkeley, measured effects of money supply on raw agricultural product prices, retail prices of food products, and the nonfood Consumer Price Index (CPI) support overshooting. Consistent with the nonneutrality of money and raw agricultural prices being generated by flex-price markets, money supply was a more important determinant--and the associated lag endogenous variable a less important determinant--of short-run changes in raw product prices than the nonfood CPI or the index of retail food prices. We have also tested the proposition that there is a relationship between the degree of overshooting and the number of flex-price markets. To perform this test, the following three regimes were defined:

Regime 1. Fixed exchange rates and fixed nominal interest rates (pre-1973).
Regime 2. Flexible exchange rates and fixed nominal interest rates (1973-1979).
Regime 3. Flexible exchange rates and flexible nominal interest rates (from the fourth quarter, 1980, through 1984).

As expected, the coefficient on money in the raw-product agricultural price equation falls as we move from Regime 1 to Regime 2 to Regime 3. In other words, for a given macroeconomic policy shock, agricultural commodity prices overshoot their eventual equilibriums more dramatically for the period 1967 through 1973 than for the later specified periods.

Trade Effects of Unstable Macroeconomic Policies

Trade and internal agricultural policies do impinge upon the total value of trade and various degrees of competitive advantage across countries; but so do various countries' macroeconomic policies. The latter policies are reflected in three major macroeconomic variables: growth rates, real interest rates, and exchange rates. The rate of growth of income is perhaps the most important of these three variables. The growth rate of income among OECD countries is a crucial determinant of the growth rate of world trade in general and of less-developed country (LDC) exports in particular. The demand for the types of goods that LDCs produce is thought to be particularly procyclical. This is why the volumes of these exports, after the rapid growth in the 1970s, fell sharply from 1980 to 1982.

LDC export volumes responded well to the U.S. recovery that began in 1983 and spread weakly to other industrialized countries in 1984. But prices of LDC exports, which began to fall during the recession, continued a downward trend through 1985, whether measured in terms of dollars or in terms of LDC import prices. Prices of LDC exports, particularly of commodities, have remained depressed throughout the 1980s, in part because of high real interest rates. The increase in world real interest rates in the early 1980s, in part a result of the shift in the U.S. mix of monetary and fiscal policy, has had three major effects on commodity-exporting LDCs. The first is a depressing effect on the price of commodity exports. The second: because much of LDC debt was either short-term or floating-rate, the increase in interest rates quickly resulted in an increase in the debt-service burden of the debtors. This was as important as the loss of export revenue during the early 1980s in the creation of increases in the current account deficit, the external debt, and the debt/export ratio. The third and final effect of higher world interest rates is the direct effect on interest rates within each LDC because of arbitrage opportunities. For many LDCs, the magnitude of capital flows in response to interest rate differentials helps explain why local LDC interest rates eventually must adjust.

This third major macroeconomic variable, the exchange rate, is influenced not by the level of macroeconomic policies but by the differences between macroeconomic policies in the United States and other countries. The pattern of influence of movements in the exchange rate on agricultural trade is indeed complex. A number of direct effects have been captured empirically. These include price effects, cross-price effects associated with substitutable commodities, and policy distortion effects (Nishiyama and Rausser, 1986).

If the value of the dollar were to increase by 10 percent, it would make very little difference to the importers of corn in Japan if the price of corn were to fall by an equivalent amount. In this instance, the net cost in Japanese yen to an importer of corn would remain the same. Throughout the early 1980s, however, with the rapid increase in the value of the dollar, the corresponding fall in the price of corn was not possible for U.S. origins since support prices were at sufficiently high levels. Because of these high levels, the so-called policy distortion effect occurred. When the price of corn from other origins is not subjected to this downward rigidity, and currency arbitrage conditions hold, the export demand facing the United States naturally falls.

There are a number of secondary or indirect effects of exchange rates that exert influence on agricultural trade. Combined indirect or secondary effects cause consequent changes in income and growth, which, in turn, affect export demand in various countries throughout the world. First, one of these indirect effects emanates from foreign central banks' systematic intervention in exchange rate markets to influence the value of their currency. When such intervention is not sterilized, it changes money supplies of the intervening countries and, in the short run, also changes the rates of income growth. Second, a change in trade balance due to movements in the value of the exchange rate will increase growth, a part of which will be spent on imports. Last, one indirect effect focuses on wealth transfers associated with current account imbalances. Current flow payments are equivalent to wealth transfers, and such transfers require movement in interest rates to restore equilibrium in money markets. These new equilibria cause changes in investment income and (ultimately) in export demand for agricultural products.

In addition to all the above effects of exchange rates, there can be additional effects on the debt/export ratio if the currency composition of the denomination of debt differs from the currency composition of exports. For example, many debtor countries suffered from the sharp appreciation of the dollar when all of their debt was in dollars while a part of their exports was in other currencies. This phenomenon occurred regardless of whether a severe shift occurred in a particular debtor country's terms of trade during the 1980s. Moreover, for this reason, the dollar appreciation has often been listed as one of the three macroeconomic shocks, along with the recession and the increase in real interest rates, that precipitated the debt crisis of 1982.

Because of inadequate domestic savings within the United States, the current and foreseeable budget deficits will continue to be a major force behind the huge trade imbalances that exist. The so-called twin deficits problem will continue to plague the export performance of the U.S. agricultural sector. Few policymakers realize that the large budget outlays of the U.S. agricultural sector are partially responsible for the dismal trade performance of the sector. The causal flow moves from subsidization of agriculture to government budget deficits to foreign countries' need to generate trade surpluses that will finance their capital flows into the United States. The latter flows provide the funds necessary to finance the huge credit demands within the United States that currently cannot be financed by internal savings.

Agriculture contributes to the trade imbalances not only through the current account but also through the taxpayer cost of agricultural programs. Because federal government deficits are partially responsible for current trade imbalances, the huge subsidization of the agricultural sector by the federal government has contributed to the U.S. trade deficit. This trade deficit has been the cause of some instability in nominal and real interest rates, as well as exchange rates, in this country. It has also contributed to political instability by providing a formal justification for protectionist trade legislation that has been actively debated by both the House of Representatives and the Senate, and opposed by the Reagan Administration. If this trade protection legislation is implemented, the U.S. agricultural sector will suffer immensely through further reductions in agricultural product exports. Hence, governmental expenditures in the short run may appear to support the U.S. agricultural sector, but in the long run could prove to dramatically harm the sector.

PUBLIC POLICY

When the government guarantees farmers a certain price or a certain income level, it absorbs risk and eliminates some of the uncertainty faced by many in the agricultural sector. Over short periods, government policy can and has succeeded in this respect. But government behavior can also create risks by contributing to commodity market instability. After the Soviet grain deal of 1972, the absence of government-held stocks contributed to large price increases. The Food and Agriculture Act of 1977 changed the commodity programs by permitting a wider fluctuation in prices. The export embargo of 1980, variations on the rules of the Farmer-Owned Reserve program since 1980, and the Payment-in-Kind (PIK) program of 1983, to name but a few major changes in government agricultural programs, make it clear that policy uncertainty can be a major contributor to private commodity market instability.

Very recently (postharvest, 1986), the major source of uncertainty in future and spot markets for nonmarketing loan programmed commodities was the outcome of the confrontation between the Office of Management and Budget (OMB) and the Department of Agriculture. The conflict focused on the percentage of deficiency payments that could be made in the form of generic certificates. The markets generally expected that if 100 percent of all payments were made in generic commodity certificates, we would in effect have a marketing loan program for corn and almost a marketing loan program for wheat. Within the bowels of government, the debate between OMB and the USDA revolved around the cost to the government of issuing generic certificates. Ultimately a compromise was reached, and 50 percent of most payments were made in the form of generic commodities certificates.

The mere existence of governments is another reason why private stockholders may not store for extreme contingencies and, thus, provide needed price stabilization. History reveals that it is difficult for governments to resist taking actions that interfere with the market system during periods of shortage. This is true of all countries--even wealthy countries, formerly wealthy countries, and soon-to-be formerly wealthy countries. In effect, market failure is induced by the simple presence of government.

Market Failure vs. Government Failure

As implied by the earlier discussion in the section on internal instability, the existence of market failure is often thought to be sufficient for justifying government intervention to correct a problem. But in addition to market failure, the effects of government failure must be considered. Government failure is the tendency of the legislative and policy implementation process to be influenced by self-interested private groups. To the extent that government intervention is captured by such groups, the public interest is not adequately served. As a result, market failure is a necessary, but not sufficient, condition for government intervention. A sufficient condition would be when the loss of economic efficiency in the case of the uncorrected market failure is greater than the loss under the government remedy, accounting for potential failures in the implementation of designed policies.

It must also be recognized that over time, policies may be modified to serve political concerns. Government policy, while perhaps achieving its direct goal, may have side effects and consequences that are unintended, unanticipated, and often costly. Once it is known that the government intends to redistribute income from one group to another, specific economic groups may lobby the government in an attempt to gain these lucrative transfers for themselves. If, for instance, the government has reduced the downside risk in producing certain commodities in accordance with the model of the appendix (PERT), farmers will specialize in these commodities since they offer a less variable rate of return than was previously the case. They will then also have an economic incentive to push for the political maintenance and extension of that government program from which they benefit (PEST).

Policy outcomes may sometimes reflect the strength of lobbies behind certain proposals--lobbies which use economic resources only to obtain income transfers for themselves, and not necessarily to work toward what is best for society. Once it is recognized that government is not a perfect instrument for correcting whatever market failure might exist, other corrective schemes must be considered. At a minimum, market failure considerations must be balanced with possible government failures. Replacing one uncertainty or source of instability with another does not necessarily lead to a net improvement.

Intra- vs. Intergovernmental Behavior

When one country pursues the seemingly innocent purpose of stabilizing its own agricultural markets, it inadvertently adds to the instability of international prices. Throughout the world, highly intrusive interventions exist with the express purpose of preventing the fluctuation of internal agricultural and food prices. When internal shortages or surpluses then develop, all of the necessary adjustments are made at the border, through changes in international trade. By making adjustments through trade, rather than through changes in domestic production and consumption, countries are forcing their own burden of adjustment onto producers and consumers abroad. They are "exporting instability" into the world's agricultural marketplace.

In essence, one country's government failure is another country's market failure. A PEST intervention in one country creates an externality affecting another country-- whether through lost markets, a lower price, or greater price instability. Intervention in one country creates conditions justifying interventions in another country, thereby leading to a further retreat from any semblance of market-determined allocation.[3]

Empirical Evidence on the International Cost of Instability

One glaring example of the international cost of industrialized-country policies is the case of sugar. Neither the European Community nor the United States has been able to adjust its sugar policies to changing economic conditions. Both the European Community and the United States have accepted increasing market distortions and dramatically growing economic cost. Moreover, because the United States has been dominant in the world sugar trade, the imposition of import quotas has depressed world sugar prices. This policy and the European Community sugar

policy have placed a great burden of adjustment on many
developing countries. One study, the World Bank's <u>World
Development Report</u> (1986), has estimated that industrialized
countries' sugar policies cost the developing countries
about $7.4 billion in lost export revenues during 1983,
reduced their real income by about $2.1 billion, and
<u>increased price instability</u> in the residual market for sugar
by approximately 25 percent.

It has been estimated that the variability of world
wheat prices could be reduced by 48 percent if all countries
were to end their ill-liberal wheat prices (Schiff, 1985).
Tyers and Anderson (1986), using a computer model which
simulates the effects of policy liberalization in more than
a half-dozen different commodity markets, have calculated
that industrial countries' liberalization of agricultural
policies would substantially reduce the international price
variability of all major temperate zone commodities--wheat
by 33 percent, coarse grains by 10 percent, rice by 19
percent, sugar by 15 percent, and dairy products by 56
percent.

Conceptually, of course, world prices could be
stabilized even if most countries were to insulate their
markets--as long as countries or private individuals
operating in free markets had sufficiently large stocks.
The size of stockpiles needed, however, increases with the
number of countries which insulate their economies. One
study of fourteen regions found that stocks had to be eight
times larger if the regions completely insulated their
economies than if they instituted free trade (Johnson and
Sumner, 1976). Clearly, the cost of extra stocks held
indicates one source of potential gain from trade
liberalization.

CONCLUDING REMARKS

The first major issue in agricultural sector stability
analysis is how large the potential benefits would be from
correcting whatever market failures exist. The second
relates to the potential failures in the government's
implementation of PERT strategies for correcting market
failures. Are the costs associated with these failures
sufficiently "small" to justify public policy correction of
particular market failures in agriculture?

It must be explicitly recognized that sources of market
incompleteness are not predetermined. Since information can
be purchased and markets opened at a cost, the sources of
market incompleteness must be isolated and the associated

costs and benefits determined for alternative institutional
designs, especially market-enhancing and nonmarket
coordinating mechanisms. Do other coordinating mechanisms
or institutions exist which improve the ability to absorb
risks by modifying the current risk-sharing across
components of the food and agriculture systems? Are private
sector coordinating mechanisms more cost effective and less
prone to PEST-related activities than governmental policy
intervention?

A major reason why a more comprehensive set of risk
markets has not arisen within the private sector can be
traced directly to heavy governmental intervention. So much
of the risk is borne (or is potentially borne) by the public
sector that private institutions have little incentive to
manage inherent instabilities and risks.

A set of issues potentially far more important than
those outlined above relates to the longer-term unstable
economic waves that have been observed for the
U.S. agricultural sector. If the U.S. agricultural sector
were only faced with short-term instabilities, the recent
crisis would not have arisen. It is far easier to design
effective institutions for managing short-term
instabilities. One to two years of unfavorable economic
conditions can be weathered, but four or five years is quite
a different matter.

History suggests that large downturns generally follow
favorable economic waves. It is indeed difficult to design
institutions and public policies to address both the
economic upturn of the 1970s and the downturn of the 1980s.
Similar waves have occurred throughout the history of the
U.S. agricultural sector, e.g., 1900-1915 vs. the 1920s and
1930s. What role have each of the potential sources of
instability--(1) internal, (2) external, and (3) government
public policies--played in determining the form and length
of the economic waves that have been experienced
historically within the U.S. agricultural sector?

APPENDIX

INCOMPLETE MARKETS AND AGRICULTURAL POLICY

To demonstrate the implications of incomplete markets,
two standard agricultural policies will be examined in this
appendix. The first is the deficiency payment, or Brannan
plan, which sets a target above the free-market equilibrium
and pays farmers the difference between this target price

(P*) and the market-clearing price (P), provided P* > P. Under this program, farmers will be presumed to choose output levels freely. The second program imposes production controls which set farmer output levels below free-market levels, thereby returning farmers a higher price for their output. The two instruments (deficiency payments and production controls) can be either combined or imposed separately. Here, we shall investigate deficiency payments both separately and in combination with production controls.[4]

Formally, consider a static, two-good economy in which the two goods are a food commodity (x) and a numeraire (y). Assume that there exists a representative (aggregate) farmer who can be characterized as follows:

1. Preferences are defined on profits and satisfy the rationality axioms of Von Neumann and Morganstern (see Borch, 1968). The representative farmer's utility can then be represented by an expected utility function, $EU(\tilde{\pi})$, where E denotes the expectation operator over states of nature, $\tilde{\pi}$ denotes the state-dependent profit, and $U(\cdot)$ denotes the ex post utility function assumed state-dependent and twice differentiable with $U' > 0$ and $U'' \leq 0$.

2. He has a production technology defined by a twice-differentiable cost function, $C(z)$ (where cost is measured in units of the numeraire), and an output function, $x = \tilde{\theta}z$, $E(\tilde{\theta}) = 1$. z is the "expected output" choice which must be made before the state is revealed, and $\tilde{\theta}$ is a state-dependent output coefficient. Assume $C' > 0$ and $C'' > 0$. Note that the cost function, C, implicitly reflects the presence of some fixed factor of production in the agricultural sector, such as land.

3. The farmer is a price taker and has rational expectations in the sense that the price he expects in state σ is the equilibrium price in that state.

Assume that there exists a representative consumer whose indirect utility function is V(P, Y), where P is the price of food, Y is aggregate consumer income, and $V(\cdot)$ is a twice-differentiable, state-independent function. Assume $V_P < 0$, $V_Y > 0$, and $V_{YY} \leq 0$. Let this consumer also obey the standard rationality axioms of choice under uncertainty so that his utility can be represented by $EV(\tilde{P}, \tilde{Y})$. Further, suppose that, in the absence of taxes to pay for deficiency transfers, Y is constant across states. Finally, assume that consumers pay the full cost of the deficiency payments via a lump sum (ex post) tax.

Suppose that there is perfectly symmetric information and that equilibrium is stable in a Walrasian sense. Further, for analytical tractability, assume that there are two equiprobable states of nature with $\theta_1 > \theta_2$; when practicable, the more general case will be examined--namely, that of states, indexed by σ, continuous on an interval $[a, b]$ with the production coefficient, $\theta(\sigma)$, decreasing in σ.

With this construction, farmer profits in state σ are:

$$\pi_\sigma = \max(P_\sigma, P^*) \; \theta(\sigma) \; z - C(z) - s_f, \qquad (1)$$

where P_σ is the market price of food prevailing in state σ, P^* is the target price, and s_f is a fixed (nonstate-contingent) government tax. When the farmer is choosing "expected output," his utility-maximization problem can be written:

$$\max_z \; EU[\max(P^*, P) \; \theta \; z - C(z) - s_f], \qquad (2)$$

with first-order condition (assuming an interior solution):

$$EU\{U'[\max(P^*, P) \; \theta - C']\} = 0. \qquad (3)$$

Clearly, the farmer's optimal z, z^*, is a function of received prices in all states, $[\max(P_\sigma, P^*)]$, the tax, s_f, and parameters of cost and utility functions. Given rational farmer expectations, market prices are determined by the equilibrium conditions (using Roy's identity and subsuming relevant parameters in the z^* function):

$$x^d(P_\sigma, Y_\sigma) = -\frac{V_P(P_\sigma, Y_\sigma)}{V_Y(P_\sigma, Y_\sigma)} = \theta(\sigma) \; z^*\{[\max(P_\sigma, P^*)], s_f\} \qquad (4)$$

where $x^d(\;)$ denotes consumer demand, assumed downward sloping in price,

$$Y_\sigma = Y - [P^* - \min(P_\sigma, P^*)] \; \theta(\sigma) \; z^*\{[\max(P_\sigma, P^*)], s_f\} - s_c,$$

and s_c is a fixed (nonstate-contingent) government tax on consumers. Letting $[P_\sigma(P^*, s)]$, $s = (s_f, s_c)$ denote the solutions to (4), the equilibrium producer input choice can be represented as a function of P^* and s alone:[5]

$$z^{**}(P^*, s) = z^*(\{max[P_\sigma(P^*, s), P^*]\}, s). \qquad (5)$$

Note that structural parameters are also subsumed in the z^{**} function.

Deficiency Payments

Define welfare in a conventional way as the sum of producer- and consumer-compensating variations (PS and CS, respectively). Essentially, government taxes are being selected to preserve agents' preprogram utilities, and the following welfare question is posed: Given P* and the associated utility preserving taxes, is there a surplus in the government budget? To answer this question for the two-state setting, PS and CS are expressed implicitly in the following equations:

$$\sum_{\sigma=1}^{2} .5\{V[P_\sigma(P^*), Y - \{P^* - min[P^*, P_\sigma(P^*)]\} \\ \times \theta_\sigma z^{**}(P^*) - CS]\} = \bar{V}^{ce} \qquad (6a)$$

$$\sum_{\sigma=1}^{2} .5(U\{max[P^*, P_\sigma(P^*)] \theta_\sigma z^{**}(P^*) \\ - C[z^{**}(P^*)] - PS\}) = \bar{U}^{ce} \qquad (6b)$$

where $\bar{V}^{ce}$ and $\bar{U}^{ce}$ denote no-program competitive equilibrium utilities of the two agents and where prices and outputs represent compensated equilibrium outcomes. Differentiating and summing for the case of $P^* < P_2$:

$$\frac{dW}{dP^*} = \frac{dCS}{dP^*} + \frac{dPS}{dP^*} = .5 \left\{ \theta_1 z^{**}(P^*) \left[\frac{U'_1}{E(U')} - \frac{V_{1Y}}{E(V_Y)} \right] \right. \qquad (7)$$

$$+ \theta_2 z^{**}(P^*) \left[\frac{U'_2}{E(U')} - \frac{V_{2Y}}{E(V_Y)} \right] \left[\frac{dP_2}{dP^*} \right]$$

$$\left. - \left[\frac{V_{1Y}}{E(V_Y)} (P^* - P_1)\theta_1 \right] \left[\frac{dz^{**}}{dP^*} \right] \right\}.$$

This last equation gives rise to:

Proposition 1: If $dP_2/dP* \leq 0$ at $P* = P_1^{ce}$, then a sufficient condition for the existence of a welfare-improving target price is that the following inequality be satisfied at the no-program competitive equilibrium:

$$MRS_{consumer} = \frac{V_{1Y}}{V_{2Y}} < \frac{U_1'}{U_2'} = MRS_{farmer} \ , \qquad (8)$$

where MRS denotes the marginal rate of substitution. Expanding and interpreting the prior condition to this proposition yields the following corollary.

Corollary 1: If (a) demand is price inelastic for $P \in [P_1^{ce}, P_2^{ce}]$, (b) farmers are strictly risk averse with nonincreasing absolute risk aversion, and (c) η (the income elasticity of demand) is approximately zero for $P \in [P_1^{ce}, P_2^{ce}]$, $Y_\sigma = Y(\sigma = 1, 2)$, then a positive target price, $P* > P_1^{ce}$, will be socially optimal.[6]

Production Controls with Deficiency Payments

When production controls and deficiency payments can be jointly employed (and we are, again, in a two-state setting), the Social Welfare Function can be written as follows:

$$W(s, P*, z^c) = \sum_{\sigma=1}^{2} .5[U\{\max[P*, P_\sigma(s, P*, z^c)] \qquad (9)$$

$$\times \theta_\sigma z^c - C(z^c) - s\} + \lambda V(P_\sigma(s, P*, z^c),$$

$$Y - \{P* - \min[P*, P_\sigma(s, P*, z^c)]\} \theta_\sigma z^c + s)],$$

where $P_\sigma(s, P*, z^c)$ denotes the equilibrium price in state σ.

Note that choice of z^c will be constrained by the condition: $z^c \leq z^{**}(P*, s)$, the producer's optimal choice in the absence of controls. Assuming that a positive target price is optimal, will this constraint be binding as the optimum? To answer this question, the first-order necessary conditions for the unconstrained maximization problem may be derived and analyzed to determine whether the constraint is violated.

With $P* < P_2$, the first-order necessary conditions for the unconstrained maximization of (9) are as follows (after some simplification):

$$\frac{\partial W}{\partial s} = [\lambda E(V_Y) - E(U')] + .5(\alpha_2\eta_2/\gamma_2)(U_2' - \lambda V_{2Y}) = 0 \qquad (10)$$

$$\frac{\partial W}{\partial P*} = .5 \; \theta_1 \; z^c(U_1' - \lambda V_{1Y}) = 0 \qquad (11)$$

$$\frac{\partial W}{\partial z^c} = E(U'[\max(P*, P) \; \theta - C']) + (\theta_2 P_2/Y_2)(\lambda V_{2Y} - U_2') \qquad (12)$$
$$- \lambda V_{1Y}(P* - P_1) \; \theta_1 = 0.$$

Now consider equation (12). The first term is the partial derivative of farmer expected utility with respect to ex ante output; if positive, production (z^c) is less than the farmer would choose in the absence of control and the constraint will not be binding. Hence, given that (12) is satisfied, a necessary and sufficient condition for production controls to be optimal is that the sum of the second and third terms be negative. A sufficient condition is that one term be negative and the other nonpositive. Since $P* > P_1$ by the assumption that a positive target price is optimal, the third term is negative and, therefore, the sufficient condition reduces to the nonpositivity of the second term. A little manipulation of conditions (10) and (11) reveals that this term must be zero; specifically, solving for λ from (11), substituting into (10), and rewriting gives:

$$.5 \; U_1'[1 - (\alpha_2\eta_2/\gamma_2)][(V_{2Y}/V_{1Y}) - (U_2'/U_1')] = 0, \qquad (10')$$

$$\lambda = (U_1'/V_{1Y}) = (U_2'/V_{2Y}).$$

Equations (10') and (12) not only imply that $E(U'[\max(P*, P) \; \theta - C']) > 0$, they are also equivalent to the conditions for a full Pareto optimum, namely, $E[U'(P\theta - C')] = 0$ and $(V_{1Y}/V_{2Y}) = (U_1'/U_2')$. It is easily verified that all of these conclusions carry over to the case of $P* > P_2$ (and of unequal state probabilities), thus proving the following proposition.

Proposition 2: In a two-state world, production controls will be an optimal complementary policy to deficiency payments whenever deficiency payments are socially desirable. Further, in this setting, the optimal deficiency payment/production control program will yield a full Pareto optimum.

In the above analysis, production controls are treated without regard to the willingness of farmers to restrain their output. When these controls are not linked to any other policy, this is a necessary abstraction. However, when both deficiency payments and output control policies are pursued, entitlement to a target price can be linked to output constraints. In this case, assuming government cannot impose controls, an additional constraint is added to the welfare-maximization problem--namely, that, given prevailing market prices with full farmer participation in the deficiency payments/control program, farmers prefer participation (i.e., receipt of the target price in low-price states in exchange for output control) to nonparticipation (i.e., receipt of market prices without control). Though this constraint may bind the government planner's choice of z^c, the following proposition demonstrates that it will not alter the implications of the above discussion with respect to the optimality of some production control.

Proposition 3: If a joint deficiency payment/production control policy is socially optimal when the government planner does not face a voluntary participation constraint, some production control will also be an optimal complement to the deficiency payment when the planner does face a voluntary participation restraint.

Proof. If the participation constraint is not binding, a production control is optimal by supposition. Now, suppose that the constraint is binding and a production control is not optimal. Participation in the deficiency payment/control program then costs farmers nothing and gives them the benefit of the target-price/deficiency payment; therefore, they will choose to participate, and the constraint will not be binding--a contradiction.

NOTES

1. The recognition of additional markets, portfolio analyses (more formally, capital asset pricing models), the size of the agricultural sector relative to the total economy and various market imperfections support the view that the risks within the agricultural sector are not totally diversifiable.

2. If overshooting does occur, inefficiencies do not arise if all agents had formed their expectations rationally in terms of the long-run equilibrium. If money is neutral in the long run and agents form their expectations in accordance with this long-run equilibrium, then even though overshooting can occur, it will not lead to any "externalities" which will generate misallocations of resources.

3. This strategic interdependence of policy creates a natural gravitation toward a prisoners' dilemma in the reform of agricultural trade. The rewards for unilateral reform are slight (as compared to the domestic political costs) when viewed beside the possible gains from multilateral reform. The incentive structure currently dictates the compounding of public policy interventions to retain markets in the face of distortions generated by other countries.

4. A more comprehensive treatment, including other policy instruments, is available in Innes and Rausser (1986).

5. The $[P_\sigma(P*, s)]$ will be assumed existent, unique, continuous everywhere, and differentiable at all points other than where $P* = P_2(P*, s)$. (At the latter points, the functional relationship between P* and farmer first-order conditions changes.) These assumptions imply that $z**(P*, s)$ is continuous everywhere and is differentiable at all points other than $\bar{P}_s^*$ which satisfy $\bar{P}_s^* = P_2(\bar{P}_s^*, s)$. (Twice differentiability of U and C implies (from the implicit function theorem) that $z*$ is a differentiable function of its arguments. Thus, the continuous and composite mapping theorems (Marsden, 1974, pp. 84 and 168) imply these properties of $z**(P*, s)$.)

6. Complete development and proofs of Proposition 1 and Corollary 1 may be found in Innes (1986).

168

REFERENCES

Andrews, Margaret S. and Gordon C. Rausser. "Some Political Economy Aspects of Macroeconomic Linkages with Agriculture." American Journal of Agricultural Economics 68(1986):413-417.

Bester, H. "Screening vs. Rationing in Credit Markets with Imperfect Information." American Economic Review 75(1985):850-855.

Bieri, J. and A. Schmitz. "Market Intermediaries and Price Instability: Some Welfare Implications." American Journal of Agricultural Economics 56(1974):280-285.

Blandford, D. and J.M. Currie. "Price Uncertainty: The Case for Government Intervention." Journal of Agricultural Economics 26(1975):37-50.

Borch, Karl. The Economics of Uncertainty. Princeton, NJ: Princeton University Press, 1968.

Bordo, Michael. "The Effects of Monetary Change on Relative Commodity Prices and the Role of Long-Term Contracts." Journal of Political Economy 88(1980):1088-1109.

Bosworth, Barry and Robert Lawrence. Commodity Prices and the New Inflation. Washington, D.C.: Brookings Institution, 1982.

Cumby, Robert and Maurice Obstfeld. "International Interest Rate and Price Level Linkages Under Flexible Exchange Rates: A Review of Recent Evidence." In Exchange Rate Theory and Practice. Edited by J. Billson and R. Marston. Chicago: University of Chicago Press, 1984.

Fama, E. and M. Jensen. "Agency Problems and Residual Claims." Journal of Law and Economics 26(1983):327-349.

Frankel, Jeffrey and Dikas Hardouvelis. "Commodity Prices, Money Surprises and Fed Credibility." Journal of Money, Credit and Banking 17(1985):425-438.

Gardner, Bruce L. "Redistribution Through Commodity Markets." American Journal of Agricultural Economics 65(1983):225-234.

----------. "Causes of U.S. Farm Commodity Programs." Journal of Political Economy 95(1987):290-310.

Greenwald, B. and J. Stiglitz. "Externalities in Economies with Imperfect Information and Incomplete Markets." Quarterly Journal of Economics 51(1986):229-264.

Hathaway, Dale E. Government and Agriculture: Public Policy in a Democratic Society. New York: Macmillan, 1963.

Houthakker, H.S. Economic Policy for the Farm Sector. Washington, D.C.: American Enterprise Institute for Public Policy Research, 1967.

Innes, Robert D. Agricultural Policy Analysis in Economies
with Incomplete Markets. Unpublished
Ph.D. dissertation, University of California,
Berkeley, CA, 1986.

Innes, Robert D. and Gordon C. Rausser. "Agricultural Policy
in Economies with Uncertainty and Incomplete Markets."
Unpublished paper, Department of Agriculture and
Resource Economics, University of California, Berkeley,
CA, 1986.

Johnson, D. Gale and Daniel A. Sumner. "An Optimization
Approach to Grain Reserves for Developed Countries." In
Analysis of Grain Reserves. Edited by David J. Eaton
and W. Scott Steele. Washington, D.C.: U.S. Department
of Agriculture, Economic Research Service Report
No. 634, 1976, pp. 56-76.

Keynes, John Maynard. "The Policy of Government Storage of
Food Stuffs and Raw Materials." Economic Journal
48(1938):449-460.

Marsden, J. Elementary Classical Analysis. San Francisco:
W.H. Freeman and Co., 1974.

Newbery, David M.G. and Joseph E. Stiglitz. The Theory of
Commodity Price Stabilization. New York: Oxford
University Press, 1981.

Nishiyama, Y. and Gordon C. Rausser. "Multiple Effects of
Exchange Rates on Import Demand: The Case of
U.S. Agricultural Trade with Japan." Unpublished
working paper, Department of Agriculture and Resource
Economics, University of California, Berkeley, CA,
1986.

Rausser, Gordon C. "Macroeconomics and U.S. Agricultural
Policy." In U.S. Agricultural Policy: 1985 Farm
Legislation. Edited by Bruce L. Gardner. Washington,
D.C.: American Enterprise Institute for Public Policy
Research, 1985, pp. 207-256.

----------. "Political Economic Markets: PERTs and PESTs in
Food and Agriculture." American Journal of Agricultural
Economics 64(1982):821-833.

Rausser, Gordon C., James Chalfant, Allan Love, and Kostas
Stamoulis. "Macroeconomic Linkages, Taxes and Subsidies
in the U.S. Agricultural Sector." American Journal of
Agricultural Economics 68(1986):399-412.

Ross, S. "The Economic Theory of Agency: The Principals
Problems." American Economic Review 63(1973):134-140.

Schiff, Maurice. "An Econometric Analysis of the World Wheat Market and Assimilation of Alternative Policies, 1960-80." Washington, D.C.: U.S. Department of Agriculture, Economic Research Service, International Economics Division, Staff Report AGES-850827, 1985.

Schultz, Theodore W. Agriculture in an Unstable Economy. New York: McGraw-Hill, 1945.

Schmitz, Andrew. Commodity Price Stabilization: The Theory and Its Applications. Washington, D.C.: World Bank, Staff Working Paper No. 668, 1984.

Tyers, Rodney and Kym Anderson. "Distortions in World Food Markets: A Quantitative Assessment." Background Paper for the 1986 World Development Report. Washington, D.C.: World Bank, 1986, Table 6.9, p. 131.

World Bank. 1986 World Development Report. New York: Oxford University Press, 1986.

7

Panel Discussion: Summary and Reactions

Bruce Gardner

To Gordon Rausser's paper, and to the other presentations taken as a group, the reactions I have which come closest to being substantive can be summarized in three points: (1) instability is not as thoroughly bad as the thrust of the conference implies; (2) the existence of incomplete or missing markets, per se, has no policy implications; (3) the papers at this conference have been more academic and less directly oriented to actual farm policies than might have been expected given the conference title, and this is good.

The idea that at least some instability is good has been expressed often before, and I am only mentioning this view because I have not heard it at this conference. Variability in production conditions and in input prices encourages farmers to try different production methods, and this experimentation can lead to progress that would never occur in a purely static world. Variability in output price encourages investment in information and innovation in marketing. Even artificially created instability can be useful in production, as in interrupting a continuous corn rotation to defeat certain insect pests, much as the seventeen-year locusts defeat predators by emerging only periodically in indigestible quantities, with a long spell between meals for a predator that wished to specialize in eating them. Grossman and Stiglitz (1980) give formal definition to the idea that price instability is necessary to provide incentives for the efficient functioning of an economy containing random variables. It would certainly be

---

Professor, Department of Agricultural Economics, University of Maryland.

a big mistake to try to suppress all price variability whenever a continually evolving and stochastic economy generates it.

There is ambiguity about the subject matter of this conference, as reflected in the usage of various rough synonyms. For example, in the Rausser paper we have conjunctions of "instability and riskiness," "disorder in and instability of," and "instability and uncertainty." Whether these are equivalencies or contrasts is not clear because none of the terms are defined. However, I do not object to this ambiguity in terminology because I don't believe that drawing out the fine distinctions between these terms would be of any use in the analysis or understanding of policy issues.

Where I do see a real gain from precision is in discussion of linkages between instability, market failure, and governmental intervention. For example, consider this point from Rausser: "Only if instability and excessive uncertainty are combined with an incomplete set of risk markets does a market failure justification for governmental intervention in U.S. agriculture exist." This sentence would be equally true if the word "only" were replaced by "not even." Following are three reasons for a market to be missing:

(1)   the costs of supplying any quantity of the service (or good) are greater than the amount that people will pay for the service; i.e., the benefits of having the market are less than the costs (for example, a futures market in lima beans, or for corn to be delivered in ten years).

(2)   the benefits exceed the costs, but externalities exist, as in environmental pollution where the market for certain pollution control devices is missing.

(3)   the benefits would exceed the costs if certain asymmetric information or enforcement (adverse selection, moral hazard) problems could be overcome, but these problems preclude the usual competitive equilibrium.

Missing markets of type (1) do not justify government intervention when what is missing is a risk market any more than when what is missing is a market for an ordinary good (carpets with built-in roach hotels). Missing markets (2) provide a rationale for governmental action, perhaps to establish property rights in environmental goods. Or, to take a different type of example, subsidies might be justified for commodity storage if storage could be shown to generate external benefits. Missing markets (3) do not provide a rationale for governmental intervention unless the government has an answer to the adverse selection or moral hazard problem. For example, there is no market for farm bankruptcy insurance, presumably because adverse selection and moral hazard are unavoidable. Too bad, because such insurance would have mitigated the farm crisis of the 1980s considerably. It does not follow, however, that the government should provide such insurance. Still, when such markets are missing and cannot economically be established by government, there is a case for subsidies in markets for substitutes for the missing service (see Arnott and Stiglitz, 1986). We require a wide-ranging benefit-cost analysis of policy alternatives in all such cases. But I do not accept the presumption that the outcome will typically be to recommend intervention, so I prefer "not even" to "only" in the quotation above.

Providing an economic analysis of any of these issues is difficult, and can only be done by simplifying the problems greatly. This leads to "academic" models that purposefully assume things that are not true. The hope is that the false assumptions bear on trivial details while the essence of the issue is preserved. This is a tricky business and to my mind the best feature of the conference is some interesting efforts in this line in the papers. Notable examples are the appendix in Gordon Rausser's paper, the treatment of commodity options by Paul Fackler, and the analysis of storage-based price supports by Brian Wright. Those hungering for practical advice will of course be impatient with such efforts. But I believe there is no substitute for careful investigations of this type before studies leading to proposals of governmental action to cure instability are even begun.

REFERENCES

Arnott, R. and J.E. Stiglitz. "Moral Hazard and Optimal Commodity Taxation." Journal of Public Economics 29(1986):1-24.

Grossman, S. and J.E. Stiglitz. "On the Impossibility of Informationally Efficient Markets." American Economic Review 70(1980):393-408.

Symposium Participants

AGRICULTURAL STABILITY AND FARM PROGRAMS:
CONCEPTS, EVIDENCE, AND IMPLICATIONS

May 7, 1987

The Velvet Cloak Inn
Raleigh, North Carolina

Welcome and Introductions:

Durward F. Bateman, Dean, School of Agriculture and Life
Sciences, North Carolina State University

Dale M. Hoover, Head, Department of Economics and Business,
North Carolina State University

Daniel A. Sumner, Professor, North Carolina State University
and Senior Economist, President's Council of Economic
Advisers; at the time of the symposium, Resident
Fellow, National Center for Food and Agricultural
Policy, Resources for the Future

Session One:

Chairman - C.E. Bishop, President Emeritus, University
of Houston, and Special Assistant to the Provost, University
of North Carolina, Chapel Hill

Presentation - Robert J. Myers and James F. Oehmke,
Assistant Professors, Department of Agricultural Economics,
Michigan State University

Reaction - Michael K. Wohlgenant, Associate Professor,
Department of Agricultural Economics, North Carolina State
University

Presentation - Brian D. Wright, Associate Professor,
Department of Agricultural and Resource Economics,
University of California, Berkeley

Reaction - Walter N. Thurman, Assistant Professor,
Department of Economics and Business, North Carolina State
University

Session Two:

Chairman - David Kenyon, Professor, Department of
Agricultural Economics, Virginia Polytechnic and State
University

Presentation - Paul L. Fackler, Assistant Professor,
Department of Economics and Business, North Carolina State
University

Reaction - Kandice H. Kahl, Associate Professor, Department
of Agricultural Economics and Rural Sociology, Clemson
University

Session Three:

Chairman - Richard D. Robbins, Head, Department of
Agricultural Economics, North Carolina A&T University

Presentation - Marshall A. Martin, Associate Professor,
Purdue University

Reaction - Randall A. Kramer, Associate Professor,
Department of Agricultural Economics, Virginia Polytechnic
Institute and State University

Presentation - Daniel A. Sumner, Council of Economic
Advisers, RFF, and NCSU

Reaction - Max I. Loyd, Professor, Department of
Agricultural Economics and Rural Sociology, Clemson
University

Session Four:

Chairman - R.J. Hildreth, Managing Director, The Farm Foundation

Presentation - Gordon C. Rausser, Robert Gordon Sproul Chair Professor, Department of Agricultural and Resource Economics, University of California, Berkeley, and Senior Staff, President's Council of Economic Advisers

Panel Discussion, Summary and Reactions - Robert L. Thompson, Dean, School of Agriculture, Purdue University; Bruce Gardner, Professor, Department of Agricultual Economics, University of Maryland; Robert Young, Senate Agriculture Committee

Other Participants:

Richard K. Perrin, Associate Head, Department of Economics and Business, North Carolina State University, assisted with organization of the symposium.

The Farm Foundation and the North Carolina Agricultural Research Service provided partial funding for the symposium; additional assistance was provided by Resources for the Future.

Erin Newton was the editor of the conference volume.